WILLIAM WE

WRITING HOME
TO DORSET FROM THE YUKON

1 8 9 8

Acknowledgements

The appearance in print of these letters, written almost a century ago by my Uncle Will, owes much to the favourable reactions of folk who had the opportunity to read them in manuscript and to the enthusiasm of his daughter, Doreen. As compiler and editor my thanks are due to them for providing me with an interesting retirement pastime – an instructive venture into the field of book production and publishing.

In this pursuit I have been encouraged by several members of the family. I gratefully acknowledge, in particular, the assistance of my wife, Peggy, with the typing, that of my sister Joan in critically scanning the draft text and that of my niece, Susan Murphy who, with Doreen, was instrumental in gathering the illustrative material.

For supplying and for permission to reproduce photographs I am indebted to and thank Mr E M Clark, Photo Archivist of the Royal Canadian Mounted Police, Ottawa; Mr Doug Whyte and Miss Lesley Buchan of the Yukon Archives, Whitehorse; and M. Diane Brenner, Archivist of the Anchorage Museum of History of Art, Anchorage, Alaska.

In connection with the concluding chapters, I thank Mr R. D. Bottomley, Manager of the Kerrisidale Branch of the Canadian Imperial Bank of Commerce, for his interest and help in obtaining permission to make use of material first published in the Bank's house journal.

I thank, too, Mr Alan Tully of S.W. Typesetters, Sidmouth for the advice which helped to launch the project and, above all, Frances Kiernan for her enthusiastic cooperation and hard work which led to its conclusion.

T.D. Sanders

WILLIAM WHITE

WRITING HOME

TO DORSET FROM THE YUKON

1 8 9 8

A DORSET MAN'S EXPERIENCE
OF THE YUKON GOLD RUSH

COMPILED AND PUBLISHED BY
T D SANDERS

All rights reserved.
No part of this publication may be reproduced or transmitted in any form or by any means, electronically or mechanically, including photocopying, recording or any information storage and retrieval system, without either prior permission in writing from the publisher or a licence, permitting restricted copying.

Copyright © 1990 T D Sanders

ISBN 0 9516608 0 2

Printed and bound in Great Britain by
Biddles Limited, Guildford and King's Lynn

Distributed by
Town & Country Books
P O Box 31, Newton Abbot, Devon TQ12 5XH

Published by
T D Sanders
Oak Gates, Hawkins Lane,
West Hill, Ottery St Mary EX11 1XG

Introduction and additional writing by T D Sanders
Design, typesetting and artwork by Frances Kiernan
Maps drawn by Paul Sanders

Contents

	PAGE
INTRODUCTION	1
ATLANTIC CROSSING	3
FIRST IMPRESSIONS OF CANADA	10
THE JOURNEY NORTH	19
ACROSS THE WHITE PASS TO LAKE BENNETT	27
SUMMER AT NWMP POST, LAKE TAGISH AND A CHANGE OF PLAN	43
MOVE TO ATLIN AND PREPARATIONS FOR WINTER	55
FIRST CHRISTMAS AT ATLIN CITY	68
CHANGES IN OCCUPATION	76
THE BANK ROBBERY AT SKAGWAY	81
CONCULSION AND REFLECTIONS	85

Will White aged 20 years

INTRODUCTION

The letters which form the substance of this book were written by a young man, William White who, in 1898 at the age of 23, left his family and home town of Bridport in Dorset to seek his fortune in the gold fields of the Yukon.

His parents were of Dorset stock. His father, Thomas White, was the son of a shipwright who, in the days when Bridport supplied most of the ropes for Britain's navy and most of her fishermen's nets, worked in the then busy shipyard at West Bay. His mother, the daughter of a baker and tenant farmer, came from the neighbouring village of Shipton Gorge.

They had a family of two daughters and three sons of whom Will was the eldest and they owned a small shop in East Street, Bridport, from which they sold glass and china. The Whites' were a happy, closely knit family and all regularly attended the Wesleyan Methodist Chapel where Mr White acted as Superintendent of the Sunday School. The boys were educated at the local Board School and Will, a year or two after leaving school, obtained employment as a junior clerk in the head office of the Post Office Savings Bank in London. He worked there for some five years. He attended the local Chapel and, following in his father's footsteps, took part in running the Sunday School.

There he met and fell in love with one of the teachers, a girl called Nell who, by coincidence, had come to London from Charmouth, a village only a few miles from Bridport. They became engaged but were in no position to marry and Nell soon returned to her family in Charmouth. Will's health was none too good and he was advised by a doctor to seek an outdoor job. Keen to make enough money to marry it was then that he decided, after consultation with his family, to try his luck in the recently discovered gold fields of the Yukon. His career up to this point had hardly equipped him for the rugged life of a prospector and one wonders how much he appreciated the dangers and difficulties involved in such an undertaking. But, optimistic and confident, he decided to risk it and, promising Nell that he would return and marry her within four years, he booked his passage to Canada on a steamship sailing from Liverpool.

Reproduced on the following pages are the letters which he wrote to his family during the first ten exciting months of his journey. Some are addressed to one member of the family, some to another, but all were intended for general family reading. Letters addressed to his sweetheart, Nell, were not kept and as a result there are occasional gaps in the story but this detracts little from their interest as a personal record of the life and times of a young inexperienced prospector.

1

Atlantic Crossing

Tuesday 22/2/98
R M S LAKE HURON
Mid Atlantic

Dear Father & Mother, sisters and brothers,

This ship is rolling from side to side and I have to cling on sometimes to prevent rolling into the scuppers. I suppose it is the fortunes of war. I am settled on the deck and doing my best to write, but it is easier said than done. I have had my spell of sea-sickness and feel alright now, but whilst it lasted I felt decidedly 'off'. It was most unfortunate that we should have started with such rough weather. We got it at its worst before we had begun to get used to it at its best. Sunday night was the worst. We had tremendous seas running; no one allowed on deck, but no one could remain there, for we shipped tons and tons of water with every wave. The bulwarks on our side were smashed in and are now under temporary repair.

The steerage passengers had a huge fright on Sunday night. It reads most ludicrous, but no doubt the poor fellows felt it real enough. Owing to the tossing and pitching of the boat, the bulkheads in the steerage gave way, and tons of coal came into the steerage so that it was covered nearly three feet deep. The steerage passengers are mostly Russian Jews and were fortunately all in their bunks, but the poor people were so startled that they commenced crying and praying and many of them put on their life belts under the impression the vessel was sinking. But although the accommodation is most wretched for all classes, the 'Lake Huron' appears to be a good boat and there is not much fear of our going to pot. I never felt anxious at all, for I was too far gone to know very much about it.

Before we left, Aunt Rebecca fastened all my buttons on my best black jacket and gave me several pairs of Uncle Ben's socks to wear over my others. She also gave me some packets of tea and a mug. On leaving, Uncle Ben gave me £5 and Aunt R £2 so I shall arrive in Vancouver with about £85 to my credit. I think I ought to do well on that, don't you?

And now I must close for the day for it is growing cold again. Good-night all. I thought of you on Sunday night and pictured you round the cosy fire singing "Eternal Father, strong to save". Mother and Nell doing a quiet weep. Never mind, prayers will be answered, you see!!

23/2/98

It was a grand evening. I walked up and down the deck in the dark almost alone. Ocean very quiet. Phosphorescence beautiful.

It was a good idea of Aunt Rebecca's to give me some tea and a mug. I have had a few good cups and enjoyed it immensely. I just put tea in the mug and take it to the cook and he puts boiling water to it, also a little milk, so it came in very handy. I am sitting here this afternoon with a mug of tea by my side, as comfortable and cosy as a cat with kittens. I am in the cabin this afternoon as the wind is too high for me to write on deck. Things take pretty much the same course. The weather is very good and we get on famous. I've eaten all sorts of things now and have no further fears. There is a chap in our cabin named Murdoch. He and I get on alright, but he is the kind of chap one doesn't care to introduce to one's friends. He was Sergt. Major in the Northwest Mounted Police.

There is a party of ten men on board. They form a syndicate, and are pushing on to Klondyke at once, via Teslyn Lake. They hope to get to Dawson about a month before any others, and I think they will do it. If so they will make their fortunes, for provisions will be short and what they carry will fetch fabulous prices. They have twenty beautiful dogs on board for the sleds, and 20 or 30 horses are to join them at Medicine Hat in Canada. They reckon their horses will fetch over a £100 each as 'beef'. I have played whist with several of the members, and am on speaking terms with the lot. This morning I had a chat with the leader. I should like to have gone up to Teslyn with them, but it is quite out of the question.

There is another very nice man on board and one that I would very greatly like to join, because I feel he is one that can be trusted. I have had one or two chats with him and it turns out he knows a London friend of mine. Perhaps you remember some years ago I told you one of my workmates at the Savings Bank had resigned and gone to join the N.W.M. Police. Well, he only remained away 6 months and then came back again. This chap on board is a Sergeant in the N.W.M. Police and I asked him if he ever came across this friend of mine. 'Manser' his name was. It seems that Manser was actually one of his recruits. In conversation he made some remarks similar to something I remembered having read in 'Black & White'. The article had referred to an interview with the Gold Commissioner at Klondyke. Perhaps you remember I told you what he had said about 5% making their fortunes and 60% making one or two thousands? Well, I got talking to him about the fortunes made at Klondyke and he told me that most statements were fabrications for he could tell almost to the dollar how much had been taken out of the ground. He then told me he was the Gold Commissioner at Klondyke last year and was on his way back there now. It turned out that he was the very man that the 'Black & White' had interviewed. He is a thoroughly decent chap and can be trusted. He got a claim last year in the far famed Bonanza Creek but it was too far up to be of use, and he didn't take anything out scarcely. Still he sold it for a fair sum to some who were prepared to risk it. He is going to have another shot this spring. Although he drew a blank last year, he may turn up trumps this time. I don't know what his movements are. I must have some more chat with him soon.

Friday 25/2/98

    Things go very slow. One day is much like another on deck; a walk, then a meal, then a chat in the smoke room and perhaps a round of whist, then another walk and meal and so on day after day. I don't expect we shall get ashore before Tuesday, perhaps not until Wednesday. We have had terrible strong winds against us ever since we left, whilst Sunday and Monday we made little or no progress at all, having nearly burst our boilers in merely holding our own. The Dr. on board is not a very nice man; some one in the steerage fell down and knocked himself yesterday and, on its being reported to him, he asked, "What class is he, Saloon, 2nd cabin or steerage?" On being told 'steerage' the fellow replied "Oh let him wait, I'll see to it by and by." Not much in favour of the doctor, eh?

    The accommodation on board is sufficient – for men. I shouldn't ever need more than 2nd cabin myself, but I would never allow either of our three girls to travel other than 'saloon'. It is very rough for girls in 2nd cabin. On a voyage people are thrown so much together, and one associates with those whom we should never think of speaking with under ordinary circumstances. The 2nd cabin men are on the whole a bad lot - a very bad lot indeed. The ladies are also a particularly poor lot. I should be sorry to have to own any of them as relations, however distant. There is one young girl about 22, married and going to join her husband in Canada. My heart aches for the husband. The way that married woman behaves with some of the men is scandalous. Of course the men are to blame to a certain extent. But when she accepts bottles of stout from one and allows another to untie her boots I think she is inexcusable. The only woman on board that I am interested in is an old Scotch peasant. Poor old soul; she is 70 years of age, and was never "awa fra hame" before. She talks broad Scotch and does hope and pray "Ta Lord'el bring us thro' safely" She is going out to her son in Canada, and nothing will ever bring her home again, if she only gets there safe. Quite an experience for the old lady.

    I feel as right as ninepence. Am often wondering how you are all getting on, and how the new business progresses. I am hoping Father and Mother are taking care of themselves. If they do that I shall not have come on this voyage in vain, but no matter how successful I may be financially, if I am to return an orphan, my success will be as wormwood and gall to me, for I shall feel that I ought never to have left any of you. I am sure some trouble will occur unless both Father and Mother are far more careful than they usually are. And Lill* and Flo* are neither so strong as I should like. They must look after themselves too. Bert* and Harold* are strong enough, but I am rather anxious to hear how Harold's ear is. Be sure you tell me how all are when you write. I shall imagine misfortunes if you don't.

Saturday 26/2/98

They have a very good cook on board. The meals are exceptionally good I should think, and there is always an abundance of everything and plenty to choose from. The bill of fare is the same as on the advertisement I sent you, and not as on the ticket. I find it very difficult to find anything to say now as one day is so much like another.

Perhaps I had better tell you what I have eaten to-day so far.

For breakfast: Two lots of porridge, two lots of curry and rice, two slices of bread, two hot rolls and butter.

For dinner: One plate of soup, two lots of harricot mutton, two lots of potatoes, one plate boiled rice pudding and one jam tart. Tea is looming in the distance and I am feeling as though I shall keep up my reputation. I am one of the two or three who go in for a second helping of most things. The stewards gazed on me with admiration long before I finished dinner. Needless to say I am generally the last to leave the table. I'm more than making up for last Sunday and Monday.

Goodbye xxx.

Sunday 27/2/98

It is a magnificent morning. The ocean is calm as a millpond and the sun as strong as in June. One of the most perfect days one could imagine. I am on deck in the sun, and am going to describe the service. Of course last Sunday it was far too rough to hold one, but this morning afforded an ideal occasion. At half past ten the bell for church rang and we (about 30) trooped into the saloon for our first Sunday morning service. The captain is a very quiet man and is I believe a good one. Anyway there seemed nothing incongruous

*Will's sisters and brothers

in his taking the parson's place. The first hymn was "Awake my soul and with the sun" and then the captain quietly and impressively read the prayers for morning service. The psalms were read alternately by captain and congregation. The lessons read were Proverbs 15 and St. Math. 7. The other hymns were "Art thou weary" and "The Church is one foundation". They were much appreciated I think. The captain rather humourously remarked after the benediction, "I think we'll dispense with the sermon this time". I enjoyed service very much. And dinner as well. We have just returned from 'stuffing'! I accounted for soup, roast rabbit, potatoes, carrots, bread, plum pudding, sauce, jam tart and an apple, so don't complain much just now.

I had a long chat this morning with the Gold Commissioner. He gave me a lot of good advice and strongly recommended me to try my luck. He still adheres to what he said in his interview and he said there was no reason why anyone could not make money fast if he once got there. That is the great question he said, how to get there. He knows the country well and with a party of friends he purposes going an entirely new and unknown route. But I could not join him even if I wished for he said his party was complete and they were all old friends – men who had fought, lived and starved together whilst in the Police and who knew just what one another were capable of. He advised me to endeavour to join a prospecting party going to the Teslyn district, as the country around there is known to be wonderfully rich in gold. He is a very decent chap, about the only one on board, barring myself. We are not in sight of land yet. I shall not be sorry when we arrive but still I am quite comfortable and could go on like this for weeks, if only I could get a letter now and again just to know how you all are. I expect it will be nearly another fortnight before you hear from me. It does seem a long time, doesn't it?

But now I must draw this to a close. I will just pencil a few lines when I land, to enclose with this, so that you will know when and where I leave the ship. At this very moment, about one o'clock, I expect most of you are at chapel, for our time is a few hours behind English, so that when I am at dinner you are having tea.

Well, I can only say that I am going to be very cautious and do the best I can. I only hope and pray you will all take care of yourselves and not worry about me. I will always try to do credit to the way in which you have brought me up. People used to tell me that if I make as good a man as my father it would be alright. To be so is the dearest wish of –

Your loving Will.
Best love to father, mother, Lill, Flo, Bert and Harold,
Yours always,
Will.

2
FIRST IMPRESSIONS OF CANADA

The next letters describe Will's first impressions of Canada as he made the long transcontinental journey by train via Montreal & Winnipeg to Vancouver.

2nd March 1898
Canadian Pacific Railway Hotel
Halifax, Nova Scotia

Dear All,

Here I am at last, and in clover too. The boat arrived at one o'clock this afternoon and, you can depend on it, this boy didn't wait long before he got ashore. I successfully passed the Custom's ordeal, which wasn't very terrible. The train for Montreal left previous to our arrival, and as there is only one train per day and the expense of running a 'special' is very great this weather, the Railway Co. have very kindly lodged us here, free of cost, the only expense being that of meals, which are most ridiculously cheap.

A meal costs 25 cents and for this you may have anything within reason, such as chops, steaks, ham and eggs, lamb cutlets etc; bread, butter, biscuits, tea, coffee, tarts, pie etc., being thrown in ad.lib. So you can quite believe me when I say I am in clover. This hotel is one of the most spacious constructions I have ever seen. They seemed to have built each bedroom as though they might want to utilise it as a ballroom or a drill hall. It is constructed entirely of wood, is lofty and well–heated with hot water pipes.

When I have finished writing I am going to take a bath and then get to bed. I was most agreeably surprised to find Halifax such a nice place. The harbour, of course, I expected to be nice, as it is generally considered to be the finest in the world with the exception of Sydney. It is indeed a beautiful harbour – quite landlocked – so that although we left a rough sea outside, the water within was as calm as a mill–pond. The view from the principal street is one of the finest I have ever seen, I think. Without the sun it would have been dreary in the extreme, but with the beautiful blue sky we have had this afternoon, it did indeed look grand. Oh that I were a poet or an artist! The sea was as blue as the sky which was almost 'Italianesque'. Across this blue strip, about half a mile, was the other shore covered with beautiful white snow. A little way up from the water's edge the hills began, covered with firs and pines – a beautiful dark green and brown colour – and then again behind this the white hilltops and the blue sky over all. Here in Halifax (a nice town built largely of yellow stone) I have not seen a single wheeled conveyance, nothing but sleighs; sleigh omnibusses, sleigh everything. They rattle along at a good rate and are usually raised about six inches, except the purely pleasure ones which stand 18 inches. The pavements are kept clear of snow, which is piled up at the side to a considerable height. There are several from the boat who landed here so I have company.

I have had a hamper packed with provisions to last me to Winnipeg. I had 2lbs biscuits (for butter) 1 loaf bread, 1 dozen boiled eggs, 1lb boiled ham, 2lbs corned beef, 1 tin salmon, 1 tin preserved chicken, 1 tin of something else – I forget what! 1/2 lb butter, pepper and salt, 1 tin plate and sundry other odds and ends, so I won't hurt for the next few days. Of course I shall get one good meal in the dining car, in addition to the above. I paid 1 dollar 3 cents for the lot, to be packed in a basket and delivered to me tomorrow morning. My train leaves at 7 o'clock tomorrow morning. It will be a long cold journey I expect as the roads here are everywhere blocked with snow I hear.

I posted my other letters when I landed but I fear you will not get them early as Canadian mails are so uncertain. I am posting this tonight via New York so you may get it earlier than the others. I hope you are all well, but I said all that on my other letters. You ought to be flattered with two letters in one day.

Best love to all,
Ever your loving,
Will

7 March 1898

Manor Hotel
Winnipeg

Dear Dad

I have reached thus far. Got here about quarter past one this morning, having been recommended to this hotel by the conductor of the train. I was dead tired and didn't take long to turn in.

The town is a large one, but I am not particularly impressed. The streets are about twice the width of West Street, perhaps more, and the houses are substantial. Still it is very flat. When I look round I want to see Colmer's Hill and Botham Wood. It seems very curious to see the train come sailing down the street. They pass through the street in just exactly the same way as our trams, and the horses seem to take no more notice of them. The stations are funny places because there are no platforms – you step right down onto the ground – unless you happen to fall down which is rather undignified perhaps, but quite necessary at times – to wit, after meal times. For there is something in this climate that makes you eat. My word, it is an expensive country, for I seem to be always at it. I have nothing but praise for the Yankees mode of travelling. It is so nice to be able to walk down through the whole train, having a chat here and a joke there just as the fit takes you. And then again, between each car there is a platform about two and a half yards in length. It is just grand to put on your hat and go out on this platform and get some real fresh air. I spent the larger portion of my journey out of doors.

The scenery from Halifax to Montreal was nothing to speak of, but was interesting because of its newness. But from Montreal to Winnipeg was magnificent. Of course the ground is covered with snow everywhere, and the rivers as well, but still it looked very lovely as thousands and thousands of trees cover the plains and hills, and these firs show up splendidly against the surrounding whiteness, their dark foliage being very effective in the sun. I don't think I have ever seen such bright moonlight nights as we are having. The air is so clear and the moon so bright that the night seems anxious to be lighter than the day.

I have been on shore six days now and the sun has been shining the whole day long each day – the sunsets being very beautiful.

I found two or three nice people on board the S.S Huron. There was a Syrian gentleman going to Vancouver to trade at the mines. He was born on Mount Lebanon and has been telling me a lot of interesting things about Palestine, which will come in useful for us in a year or so. He fought in the Greek war against the Turks and is banished from his native land. His people were big folks I think, but the Sultan seized all their belongings and banished them. They barely saved their lives. The poor chap doesn't like to talk of it. Then there was a Mr and Mrs Macfarlane from Scotland. They are going to Vancouver where they have a brother living.

From what I hear, accommodation in Vancouver doesn't exist at all. People are sleeping in the open on shutters or anything they can find. Mr Macfarlane has given me his brother's address and is going to see after some shelter for me before I arrive. They are very religious - awfully shocked and horrified at my speaking of 'Sunday'. "Do you mean the Sabbath?" one of them solemnly asked me. They are nice homely people however, and I spent many happy hours with their daughter. Perhaps I had better make it quite clear that the said daughter is between three and four years of age. (That will be a weight off Nell's mind).

I have been obliged to get a pair of Arctic rubber boots lined with flannel, with felt uppers, to wear over my ordinary boots. They are wonderfully warm and quite watertight. Cost 97 cents. Leather boots are no good at all in getting about amongst the slush.

I believe I am very fortunate again. I called upon the Government Agent here – Mr Haslett's friend, and had a long talk with him. The result being that he has given me a letter of introduction to Mr Mann asking him to assist me. Mr Mann suggested that I might try and join Mr Stansfield's party but I don't suppose there will be any opportunity to do so. I don't think I should altogether care about it. They will no doubt do well, for the leader is a smart fellow and the party splendidly equipped. But Stansfield is a funny man to live with. He is too fond of 'bossing' and many of the party are men who have never had a master over them but have led a life as free and independent as himself. Hence 'ructions' abound. If one is content to obliterate oneself, all is well, but I can't do that myself. I might get him to carry my year's outfit though, in return for my assistance. He has the matter under consideration, but it is very doubtful I think.

Your letter reached me yesterday, Nos. 3 and 4, both arrived together; one four days late and the other two days. The mails are disorganised now owing to heavy floods.

I am so sorry to hear dear Mother is not up to the mark, I do hope she isn't given to worrying about me. It is so unnecessary for I'll be alright.

Sunday 20th March 1898

In the woods on the estuary of the Forest River, B.C.
About 3 miles from Vancouver

My dear Lill,

It is your birthday next, so I must address this week's effusion to your worthy self. I hope this will reach you in time and find you as well and hearty as it leaves me. I am having quite a new experience! You will see from the heading of this sheet that I have changed my address. I have specified my whereabouts as plainly as I could. My week at the "Norden Hotel" expired on Friday and Mr Stansfield very kindly told me that if I cared to save the hire of a room I might occupy one of his tents just to take care of it. Mr Stansfield is the leader of the party that came over on the Lake Huron. You will remember I said I hoped I might join them. We are camped almost down on the beach, so close that I could easily throw a stone into the sea from the centre of my abode. It is quite a large tent - stands about 10 feet in height and easily accommodates 14 men. I have it all to myself, the other members of the party occupying a log cabin about 20 yards away. There is another similar tent about 20 yards off, and the lady nurse, en route for Klondyke, is going to take up her residence in this. We all have our meals in the log cabin and our own cooks etc. I board with the party paying 45 cents per day. This is much less expensive than living in the Town at 25/- per week. We live very well indeed. This morning for instance we had the following assortment on the table for breakfast: Bacon, fried sprats, fried chops, salmon, preserved apricots, marmalade, bread, butter and coffee. Not bad, I'm sure.

Yesterday was washing day. Ta-ra-ra-ra-boom-de-ay. It was a sight for the gods! You should just have seen your brother washing shirts and - well, 'other articles' and then to see the graceful way he hung them out to dry!!! Oh it was just 'superb'. Never mind, they all dried very nice, anyway. Never mind if I have got to wash them again tomorrow! The fact remains that I did wash them, at least they were all very wet. And I like this rough and ready mode of living. It is great fun! I have spent two nights under canvas now. It doesn't take us long to 'turn in' at night. We find no necessity to put our hair in curl papers. Just pull off our boots and jacket, spread our blankets and roll ourselves up in them. That is all the operation. I have made myself a very soft bed to lie on, by cutting dried bracken of which there are large quantities here. I wear a pretty dark green sweater, so have discarded collars and cuffs, which seem very little in vogue in these regions.

Stansfield has lent me one of his dogs which I have chained to the centre post of the tent. I can thus leave everything without any anxiety of its being sneaked. At night I sleep with the dog at my feet and a loaded revolver by my side just within reach. It is a nice healthy life this! You get so much of the open air, to say nothing of snakes. I dreamt of snakes last night.

You will excuse this bad writing won't you for I dreamt my fingers were swollen by a snake bite. They abound here. I saw two yesterday and heard half-a-dozen rustling through the leaves. This morning I came across another. I would have killed the beggar if I had had anything in my hand. Those I have seen have not been very large, about 2 feet in length, and of a dark green colour. What a change from 5 weeks ago when I spent Sunday camped at *Worcester House.

---

*Just before Will left for Canada his family moved from the small shop in East Street to a larger house in West Street. Part of the ground floor had been converted into a shop from which it was planned to sell, not only glass and china, but second-hand furniture, antiques and books purchased at local auction sales. They renamed the house Worcester House.

Tuesday 22nd March 1898

My dear old Lill,

I intended to have written you such a long letter on Sunday, but circumstances prevented. My plans at present are more decided. There was a big row at the camp. A Mr Myers, one of the staunchest and straightest men in the party, a retired farmer, who roughed it in Canada for 12 years and made a fortune, joined the party just before leaving Liverpool. He has been living in Yorkshire, but the old instinct has got strong in him again and he felt he wanted to have a good old roughing time again, so made up his mind to go north. He has always been my favourite, not only because of his general ways, which are rough and hearty as you would expect from a farmer, but also because of his integrity. One instinctively feels he is as straight and genuine as "they make em". On Sunday Stansfield set the men to work just as on any other day. Old Myers took no notice of his instructions, and Stansfield soon noticed it and wanted to know why he didn't get something to do. Myers turned on him and said: "Mr Stansfield, I've been a farmer for 40 years. Often my heart has been sore when I've seen my wheat and my hay spoiling because I wouldn't haul it on a Sunday, but sir, I'd rather the whole crop spoiled than do unnecessary work on the Sabbath". And the old man wouldn't work and didn't. Stansfield bullied him yesterday about something and Myers could stand it no longer. He just said he would draw out his share from the Company, and have no more to do with it. Today he received his money and has asked me to accompany him on a prospecting expedition north. I have consented and we shall soon be off. It is a lucky thing for me because the old man is well experienced in roughing it; is as nice a man as I could wish, as warmhearted as anyone I know. When he first asked me to accompany him I refused because I knew he had a lot of money with him and thought he would lay in a more expensive outfit than I could manage. But he told me I had quite sufficient, because a great many things he would have to get would do for both of us, such as tent, boat, stove, tools etc. He is not going to spend anything like all his money so we shall be alright. I expect we shall go up on the Pelly River. Go through Teslyn Lake, down the Hootalinqua River to Fort Selkirk, and then up the numerous creeks on the Pelly. They say it is very rich country there. But we haven't quite decided yet. Anyway, don't send any more letters to

Vancouver please. I will tell you on my next letter where to write if it is possible.

We are going to get the best part of our year's provisions from the Hudson's Bay Co. here and get them to forward them on to their nearest depot. This will save a great deal of hard work and we shall be able to fetch them when we want them. We shall go in light with about 4 months provisions; take a boat with us, also a tent and probably 2 horses.

Well, my dear girl, I am afraid you will consider me very selfish, talking so much about myself, but it is such an interesting subject on which to expatiate that I get carried away. I have just been getting some of the ginger biscuits you put in my kit bag. I wish the kit bag was full of them. I can make very nice biscuits now – you try them: one quart of flour, a teaspoon of baking powder, mix some water and get it into a thick paste; cut into squares and put in the baking dish to bake. Be sure you don't mix into a stiff dough for, if you did, they would not be the same as mine.

I am glad to hear that Pater is better and that the sale was a success. I liked the advertisement in the Bridport News. I am glad the shop will not be utilised for second-hand furniture. I think that would lower the class of shop altogether. Furniture will go first rate in the store tho'.

I am glad Father and you girls can enjoy a game in the evening. It makes it so much less trying for Dad to cease studying business. I thoroughly believe in 'business for business hours' and I don't think he ought to let it encroach so much upon time that ought to be devoted to recreation.

I went to Baptist Chapel on Sunday evening, as the preacher advertised a special sermon for those going north. The poor man was very earnest, but had not the power to interest. He felt it badly, for when, after a long sermon, he came to 'lastly', he said, "Now, do please attend to this point whatever else you have missed – I know I have sent half of you to sleep, but you must wake up now. D'ye hear what I say? Wake up! Get up and stretch yourselves if you like, only don't miss this next point."

Trains are very late just now, so consequently the mail is. For instance, yesterday's mid-day train isn't expected to turn up until sometime tomorrow. But the good folk of these parts say that isn't bad at all. I don't like to ask what they consider 'bad'.

And now dear, goodbye. Don't forget to look after yourself, mind. With very best wishes for many happy 21st birthdays and fondest hopes for future happiness and with very best love to you and to all

From your affectionate brother Will.

P.S. I have just been looking at your photo and the more I see of it the better I think it. It looks very natural and I like it muchly.

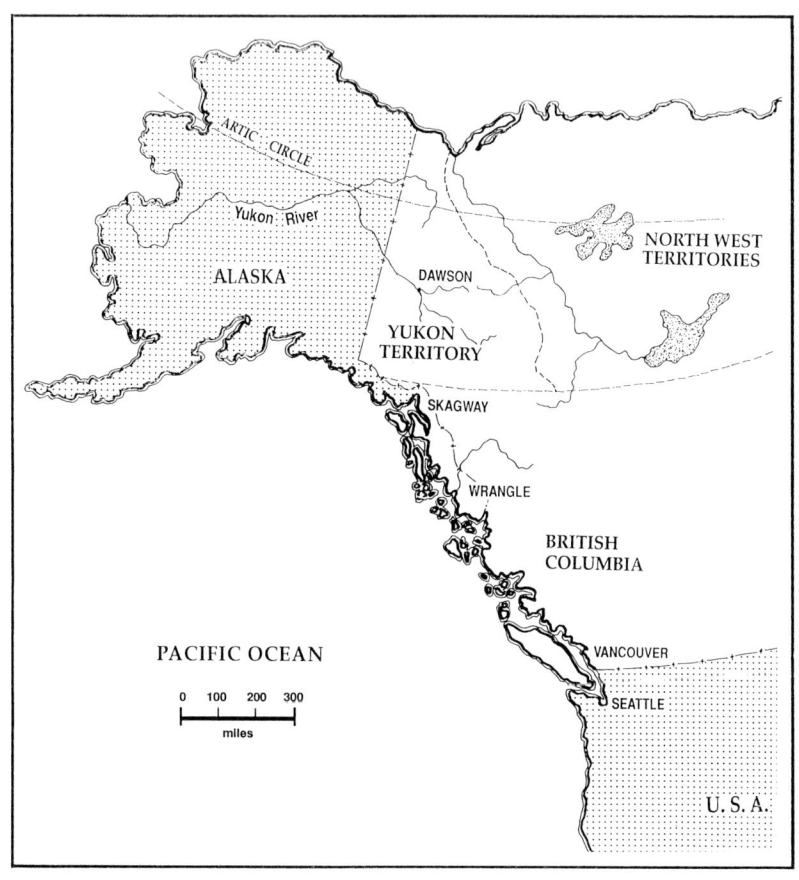

3

THE JOURNEY NORTH

    The goldfields were situated more than 1000 miles north of Vancouver, not far short of the Arctic Circle. The richest discoveries had been made among the creeks of the Klondike river, a tributary of the great Yukon, which it joined at the shanty town of Dawson. To reach this area from Vancouver and other ports along the western coast of America most of the hopeful prospectors chose to follow the shortest and most direct route. This first involved travelling by sea to the small ports of Skagway or Fort Wrangel situated in the narrow strip of American territory known as the Alaskan Panhandle. They were then faced with the enormous task of crossing the coastal mountain barrier but, once over it, they could, when the spring thaw came, complete the rest of their journey on water, travelling down the 500 odd miles of lakes, rivers and rapids to Dawson.

    Will chose to follow this course and took passage on the *Ningchow*, an old tramp steamer brought over from China in the early days of the stampede to join the fleet of motley craft assembled to ferry the prospectors north.

30/3/89
S.S. Ningchow
Pacific Ocean

My dear Florrie

I am sadly afraid your birthday will have passed ere this reaches you, but I hope you won't think you are overlooked. I had a letter half written in my case when these new arrangements of which you may have heard made me too busy to complete it. I suppose everybody will be anxious to know just what I am doing and where I am migrating to now. Well, Myers began to get half hearted about going and will probably return to England. I had another chat with Stansfield and arrangements were being made for my becoming one of the company with £70 in £1 shares as my portion:- i.e. £50 cash down, and the £20 for expenses since leaving England. The idea of the company is that 9 or 10 men are likely to drop across at least one good claim and of course if one of them turns out real good it will make the fortunes of the lot. The idea is a good one, but I am not a member and on reflection I am glad of it. Just before the matter was to be decided Stansfield got arrested because he refused to take the nurse, Gladys Egerton. The end of the affair was he has to take the nurse and pay £25 law expenses. That put an end to all the negotiations for my joining them. Yesterday morning about three and a half hours before the Ningchow sailed, Stansfield told me he would offer no objections to my journeying with them and as he had secured a special rate for passage and freight I might join the company for the voyage. This meant I should save 30 shillings; that I should be amongst a nice set of fellows with whom I have been ever since I left England; that I shall have pleasant travelling companions on the trail; adequate protection and good guidance and help always at hand, right up to the Big Salmon River. Moreover, when I get there, all I find will be my own, and I am quite my own master all the way on. I have my own tent and shall pitch it by the side of theirs. It is not decided yet whether I board with them or not. I shall try and do so, because it will save so much trouble on the journey, and I shall then have my provisions intact when I get there. Well, I made up my mind to seize the opportunity and here I am. I enclose a list of what I have bought. There are a few odd things such as tools, cooking utensils etc. that I can get at the depots up the river. The cost will be a mere trifle, whilst they would be cumbersome to take, especially if I arrange to board with Stansfield.

I find I have eighty six and a half dollars (£17.5s.0d.) in hand, so am doing well, as all expense is now practically at an end.

It is not decided which route we take. We land at Wrangel to see what the trail is like. If the ice is good we shall let the dogs take us up to Glenora (Fancy me, clad in furs, sat in a sleigh, driving a pair of dogs.) From thence we shall pack across to Teslyn Lake. But the ice may be in bad condition, in which case we shall go on to Skagway, for which place our tickets are available, and thence over the White Pass and 50 miles further to Teslyn. I hope we shall take the latter as it is so much shorter.

I have about 800lbs to take over, but can manage it by going about a dozen times or less. I daresay I shall finish long before the company have, for their outfit is many tons in weight, and even with 7 donkeys it will take them several days to get across the Pass. My freight bill was 6 dollars but theirs amounts to 558 dollars (£110) so you can see they have a task. Once over the Pass it will be child's work getting the things to Teslyn Lake. Will you send this on to Nell, but you need not send the list of additional outfit as I have told her.

31st March 1898

About 5 o'clock this evening we commenced to go through the grandest scenery imaginable and we are still in the midst of it, but unfortunately it is dark now. We are passing between countless islands and the mainland. The islands are covered with high hills and are just one mass of trees, whilst the mainland rises abruptly from the water's edge into snow-clad mountains. Often the channel is not more than 100 yards wide.

I am sorry Nellie was unable to sing at your concert. Never mind better luck next time.

Nellie will give you all the information about writing me. You will be interested in knowing that I am growing a beard. It is coming out thick, according to latest calculations there are fully 29 distinct hairs, averaging in length from one eighth to decimal 00000000 of an inch. And it hasn't stopped growing yet either!!!

We had a grand scare at the Camp just before leaving Vancouver. We were awakened about 1 o'clock by the dogs. I never knew them so excited. The whole 23 of them were yelping themselves into a state of madness. To make matters more exciting we distinctly heard the thud of a heavy tread and the loud 'sniffing noise' an animal makes when smelling. I had my head outside of the tent in no time but the other fellows were before me; then the loud report of two revolver shots close at hand sent me deep down into the furs again where I remained in fear and trembling till daylight, thinking of course, that the sneaking Indians from the Reserve nearby were on the war-path and meant to tommyhawk me. Imagine my disgust the next morning to find that it was only a bear from the woods nearby. The fellows fired at it but in the darkness Bruin got away. They heard him crashing through the bush and his tracks were visible, but no blood marks, so I suppose he was not hit. The chaps made rare fun of me. We see lots of strange things out here, but it would take too long to write every little incident.

I am enjoying the trip immensely but there is hard work just ahead. I am ready for it and impatient to begin. I was never in better trim for work. The members of the company all say how much fatter and healthier I look than when I left Liverpool.

31st March 1898

We are about 18 hours from Fort Wrangel and the air is now beginning to get much cooler. One feels it and we shall soon have to get into warmer clothes. It rains a great deal, but that makes no difference as I am quite invulnerable in my yellow oilskins. I quite fancy myself decked out in a long yellow oilskin coat. When I say long it only means that it is down to my knees. No one thinks of wearing a coat longer. For one reason long boots makes it unnecessary; but the chief objection is that it impedes walking, especially when one is carrying a load thro' slush. I should cut Father's coat off if it were likely to be of use but everyone tells me it is useless for that climate. I have found that it does not keep the wind out, especially whilst we were crossing the prairies. I am going to leave it at Wrangel, together with several other things which it is useless to carry. Every pound of useless luggage will be a relief, and old-timers know just what it is useless to take. I shall leave it with one of the company (Mr. Swan). The Company have bought a hotel there and sent on one of its members to manage it. I expect I shall have my letters sent to him, but cannot say yet.

And now I must dry up. Don't worry or let anyone else worry about me. I don't feel at all less confident of the result of all this. On the contrary, if everyone will only take care of themselves I'll eat my Christmas dinner at Worcester House in 1899.

I am so glad the new business promises so well.

Now then just remember, the one who doesn't take care of him or herself shall not have a nugget.

With fondest love to each and all,
Ever your loving brother Will.
Love to Lill and Mother.

Particulars of outfit in addition to kit taken from England
1 tent (8 x 10). 1 sled. 1 shovel. 1 pick. 1 gold pan. 55 feet rope. 1 candlestick. 1 box cartridges. 1 fur robe. 1 fur overcoat. 1 pair Wellington boots. 2 pairs moccasins. 1 ground sheet. 1 pair rubber hip boots. 2 pairs woollen stockings. 1 suit (lined) canvas clothes. 1 mackinaw coat. 1 heavy sweater. 1 pair mits. 1 pair lined mits. 1 pair drawers (chamois leather). 1 oilskin bag. 1 fur cap. 1 sleeping cap. 1 oilskin coat. 200 lbs flour. 78 lbs oatmeal. 77 lbs bacon. 25 lbs evaporated potatoes. 10 lbs onions. 25 lb evaporated apricots. 10 lbs coffee. 5 lbs tea. 5 lbs cocoa. Half dozen baking powder. 10 lbs salt. 1 lb pepper. Half pound of mustard. 5 lbs butter. Half dozen condensed milk. 5 lbs soap. 1 box candles. 1 tin matches. 50 lbs beans. Cooking utensils, odds and ends etc., I can get later on before finally parting with civilisation.

4 April 1898

Skagway, Alaska

My dear Mother

I'm quite sure it is time you had a letter from me, and if you get the letter from Wrangel and hear of the dreadful affair in the Chilkoot you will be very anxious to know whether or not your boy was near. It only happened last night and the consternation here is very great as the scene of the disaster is less than 5 miles away. The latest reports say there are 100 killed. The first thing we heard when we got in port this morning was that 200 had perished. By all accounts the Chilkoot is a terrible place and I don't mean to ever test it. I am very pleased with Skagway. It is romantically situated deep down between very high mountains covered with snow. Of course things are very primitive, as in all new towns, but it is at least clean. Wrangel must be about the dirtiest, filthiest, wickedest place on God's earth.

Between Wrangel and Skagway we had a very rough passage and I was sick for about an hour but didn't miss a meal, so you can guess I wasn't very bad.

I have some exceptionally good news for you this time. The members of the Southport Yukon Syndicate Limited with a capital of £4,000 nominally but in reality an unlimited sum behind them, unanimously voted that I should be admitted into the Company. So that I am now on an equal footing with the rest of the members. We are each promoters of the Company which will be formed next year to take over the proceeds of this Syndicate. It is not decided what amount I can put into the company. They take over all my outfit and reckon my expenses from Liverpool and what money I have so that it will be about £70 in ordinary £1 shares. In the event of my falling sick, they assist me back to civilisation and my £70 then becomes preference shares at 20 per cent. We are nine of us, each able to take up claims; if only one of these turn out good, it means that there will be no difficulty in making a few thousands each whilst, if we are more fortunate and find several good claims, we shall turn over some money.

We are splendidly outfitted. Any amount of comforts, not to mention luxuries. In fact we have about 1500 lbs of provisions for each man. Any amount of the best clothing. Six donkeys, 1 mule, 23 dogs, two splendid canoes, and 1 boat. If you only knew just how everything is you would see that it is a splendid piece of luck for me. I cannot possibly lose a cent if the whole thing turned out a failure, which is out of the question considering what men we are.

We intend to take the White Pass very easily. Probably we shall be in this neighbourhood three weeks, as it will take us quite that time to travel the 18 miles to the summit. It will be stiff work. I am very happy and contented with my success so far.

We have already started so cannot stay to complete.

Write again in a few days.

Writing about this journey several years later Will gave a more graphic description of his reaction to events.

After spending a couple of weeks in Vancouver, outfitting for the north, I sailed on an old tramp named the Ningchow loaded to the gunnels, and in due course landed at Skagway, having thrown in my lot with a party of 8 – all Englishmen – en route. To a youth from a God-fearing home in England the transition to the wild and woolly was a tremendous experience. What with the drinking, gambling, hourly brawls and nightly orgies, the tinhorns and the floosies, there was enough evil on that boat to stake a sub-section in Hell, and a vivid incident I saw as we were leaving the port of Wrangel convinced me that I was indeed a long way from home. The lines were casting off when a section of the crowd on the wharf, threw themselves flat, or ran, and simultaneously a couple of shots rang out. I saw one man crumple up and lie flat – another, with a smoking gun in his hand, approached him, prodded the body with his foot and walked away behind a shed with an ugly snarl on his face. Our boat was on the move and I never heard what it was all about but it made me realise that I was in a new world. On arriving at Skagway I was leaning against a pile of cases on the wharf, awaiting shipment, when someone asked me if I knew what was in 'them boxes'. I said I did not and was horrified to hear him say, "Them's corpses." A short time before there had been a big snow slide at Sheep Camp on the Chilcoot Pass a few miles away, in which 60 lives were lost and 'them boxes' contained the bodies of some 10 of the victims that were being shipped south to their homes for burial.

Skagway, in 1898 and '99 was probably the greatest sink-hole of iniquity the North American Continent has ever known – a fact borne out by many contemporary writings. Wild and lawless beyond conception, the infamous Soapy Smith and his gang were in full control, and robberies and killings were of nightly occurrence. High-powered crooks and denizens of the underworld plied their calling brazenly and with impunity, for the U.S. Marshall was their friend and got his 'cut' from all.

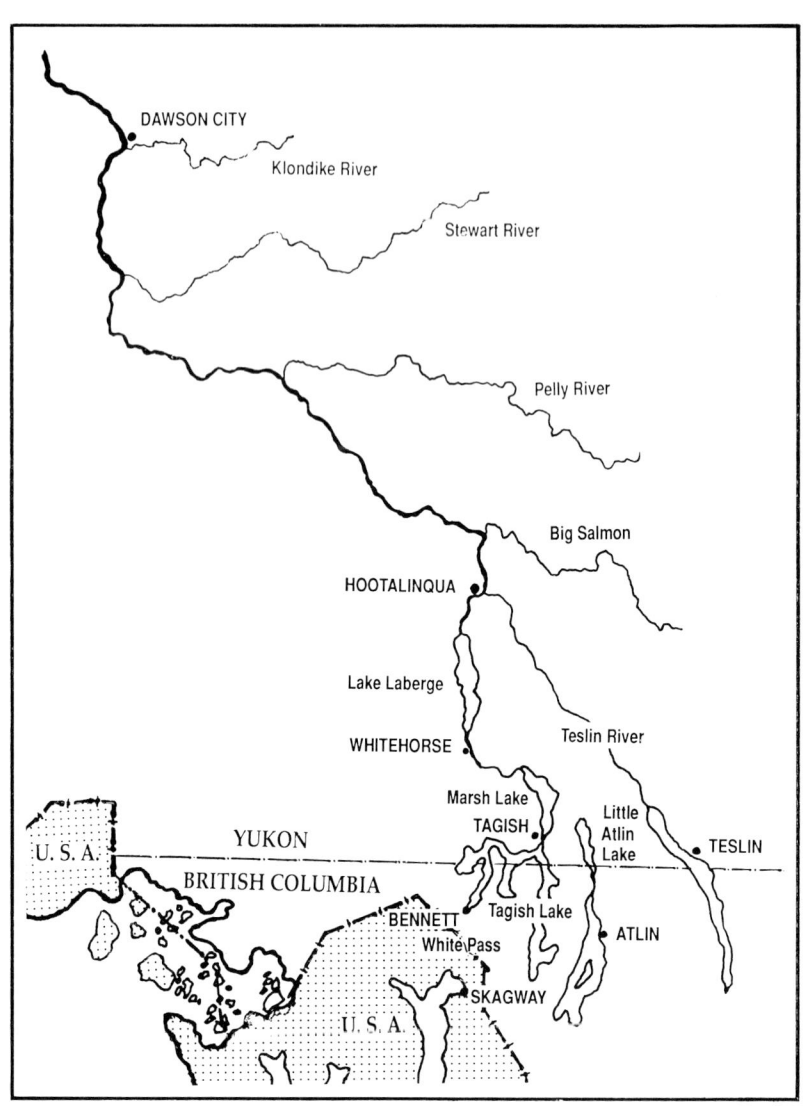

4

ACROSS THE WHITE PASS TO LAKE BENNETT

Will was now faced with the most daunting part of his journey. Skagway lay between steep hills at the mouth of a small river valley. The trail, blazed many years before by Indian trappers and traversed during the previous year by thousands of stampeders, made its way up the valley for about 20 miles to the White Pass over the mountain barrier. The Pass was nearly 3000 ft. above sea level and marked the border between Alaska and British Columbia. There the N.W.M.P. had established a customs post and only prospectors equipped with goods sufficient to enable them to survive for twelve months were allowed to proceed.

Faced with the task of transporting many hundreds of pounds of goods up this very rugged rocky trail, animals of all kind were pressed into service. Many failed to make it and the track was strewn with their corpses.

(Many prospectors favoured an alternative slightly shorter route over another pass, the Chilcoot, but this was impossible for animal transport. Prospectors had to carry their goods on their backs or hire 'packers' to do so.)

From the top of the pass the trail led down onto the Yukon plateau, a vast barren region of mountains, forests and glaciers interlaced with lakes and rivers which formed the headwaters of the Yukon river. The prospectors first objective was Lake Bennett – some ten miles on. There they built makeshift boats or rafts and, when the ice melted in the spring, they took to the water to begin the long 500 mile journey through lakes and rivers to Dawson and the Klondike gold fields.

10th April 1898
Twixt Summit of White Pass & Skagway
Mother's birthday

Dear Mother and all,

You will be glad to hear that I am still alive and kicking though circumstances are combining to try and make me otherwise. Several of our members have been knocked up, but I am as lively as a cricket. The past week has been a scorcher, and our strength has been tried to the utmost. When night has come we have simply been too tired for anything except to tumble on to our blankets and sleep as we fell. But it is not the work that has 'knocked' a few of our members. We have been camped for four days in a swamp and the air, especially at night, is very very damp. We are straining every nerve to get out and have been working hard all the morning, packing the stuff up the trail. We hope to strike camp tomorrow morning, and our next camping ground will be at the foot of the hills leading to the summit. I took a 50 lb bag of flour over there this morning.

It is a nice dry healthy spot, but we hope to be on the summit by Tuesday or Wednesday. This trail is awful! Had we been a month earlier, or had the Spring been even moderately cold, we should have gone up the river on the ice, and the dogs would have come in nicely. But the ice is almost done for and it isn't safe to journey on. I was taking a dog team with a sled load on Good Friday, but fell through the ice three times. Fortunately, I had on my rubbers up to my waist, so didn't get wet and as the sled was only loaded with flour it didn't matter. The outer flour, of course, gets wet but it then forms a paste and protects the other.

Some of the others were less fortunate, being overtaken by the dark and having to abandon dogs and sleds about a mile from the cache. We found all the dogs the following day and managed to rescue the sleds and contents, with half a day's work in a snowstorm. They have constructed what they fondly call a waggon road, but that is a libel on roads. Take a stretch of the cliffs from West Bay to Lyme Regis and cover it the whole distance with the stretch of beach between Eype and Seatown, and you get some faint idea of what this "waggon road" is like. It is rough work and a rough time for all of us, but it is doing me good. If you saw me you would be glad I had come, for the work is making me look more like I used to want to look.

I am very glad I joined this party. I feel quite a somebody as I look around and see all the tons of stuff and the donkeys and dogs, and know that they belong to me partly. We are all equals here - nine of us. Stansfield, gentleman and leader; Colley, civil engineer; Wilson, sportsman; Porter, carpenter; Swann, horseman; Williams, cook; Norris, yachtsman; Young and myself, bossing the lot. We have grand times here sometimes. Camp life is a huge joke even when it is in a swamp. I shall have some fine yarns to spin when I get back next year. I have not had my shares allotted as yet. We have been so busy that there has been no opportunity of going thro' matters.

Oh dear, what an Easter Sunday. The cook has just been to say that one of the dogs has run away with 10 lbs of beef which was to have been roasted for dinner. When the boys get back they'll either murder the cook or the dog.

And now I must dry up and write to Nellie.

Your loving son Will xxxxxx

24th April 1898

Skagway

Dear All,

Just a line. You will wonder at me writing from here. I will just explain. We have our main camp 9 miles from the summit of White Pass, i.e. the other side, but Swann remained in charge of the donkeys at a camp about 5 miles this side of the Pass. He had a hired packer to help him. Yesterday afternoon I left our camp to go down to Swann and pay the packer. I got there about 8 o'clock after a tramp of 14 miles right through the Pass, but the packer had not turned up with the donkeys. We waited until 10 o'clock, but no donkeys and no packer arrived. We then found his bag was missing, so we concluded he had bolted with our six mokes. We wrapped up in rugs and had a short nap and at half past three this morning started down the trail towards Skagway 14 miles distant, whilst Swann made off in the other direction of the head camp to tell of the robbery. On the road I learnt from three sources that the packer had been seen here yesterday afternoon trying to sell the donkeys. I can find no trace of him or the animals tho' they must be here somewhere as they passed the toll gate and no boat has left. The only law official is away, so there is nothing to be done until I hear from camp. Probably Stansfield will be down this evening. I shall drop here tonight anyway. Fortunately I have about 80 dollars of the Company's money with me.

I am having some exciting experiences. Last Sunday I and the 6 donkeys were placed under arrest by the US Customs official owing to some breach of regulations. I was released in about three hours, none the worse. Of course I was not taken to gaol, only forbidden to leave Camp. I had a big bother the other day with the mule. It fell sick whilst out with me. Had I my revolver with me I should have shot it, but I had left it at camp some miles off. On reaching camp I was too tired to go back, so Norris went, but when he reached the mule it was dead.

9 o'clock

I made up my mind to find those donkeys, so after dinner I began a thoro' search, going into saloons and still more questionable places, until at last I ran my man to earth. I never lost sight of him again till Wilson arrived about seven and he has all the management of the case. Such a thing as law doesn't exist here, so as long as we get off with the mokes we shall not bother with the man.

I am quite used to the White Pass, having crossed it between twelve and a dozen times. We feed well still, having bacon and beans six days a week and beans and bacon on Sundays for a change.

I am feeling better than I can ever remember; the outdoor life up here amongst the mountains making me stronger every day.

I am as brown as an Indian they tell me, for I cannot see, such a thing as a looking-glass being unknown. As a rule I only manage to wash my face once a week, but now and then I manage to get it done twice in seven days.

I shall be going back to the camp this side of the Pass tomorrow early and on to the chief camp the following day, so I want to get to bed early and have a good long rest. We expect Colley back from Vancouver in a few days and oh I am anxious for my letters. I know there will be a big budget for me.

And now night night Daddie, Mammie, Nellie and kiddies all.

Your affectionate son, Will

(Cheer up Nellie dear)

25th April 1898

Badminton Hotel
Skagway

Dear Father and Mother,

You will be glad to hear further from your wandering boy who, unlike the prodigal, although he has spent all his substance in a far country, does not think of returning to his home – not anyway yet.

Wilson couldn't manage to get the donkeys so has gone for Stansfield who cannot possibly reach here till tomorrow night. I am remaining here to see that the donkeys are not neglected or sneaked.

I think I remarked on last night's letter that I was very brown. This morning I was able to see my phiz in a real looking-glass and really I didn't recognise the creature. I found myself confronted by a nut-brown animal with quite a beard and a moustache. When I last saw myself about 3 weeks ago I was a pale smooth faced alabaster doll sort of chap. Hard work and mountain scenery seems to suit my constitution. All our party are well again. Two others and myself are the only ones who have borne the strain of the Pass without getting really bad colds. I got a troublesome sniffing cold in the head, but it went no further and soon passed off.

The scenery of the mountains is grand. Of course we have to wear snow glasses constantly, so we see thro' coloured spectacles and things may not be as beautiful as they appear. I think you would appreciate the scenery tho' Spring has set in, but although the temperature in the sun is as much as 70° to 80° in the daytime the snows are not melting as the frost is so severe at night. One night up at Balsam City the thermometer registered 20° below zero – only last week. I didn't feel it much colder than usual. It seemed very frosty and I noticed my moustache was covered with icicles. Had there been a breath of air, of course we should have had an uncomfortable time, but the night was perfectly still. We are camped on several feet of snow. We cut down balsam trees and split them so as to form a floor; the boughs form good beds upon which we spread many blankets and sleep as cosy as you could wish. The balsam has a pleasing healthy odour with it.

I have just bought Lloyd's Weekly News for the 3rd inset. It has just arrived by a steamer, and I had to pay 15 cents for it, and am glad to get it at the price. It seems nice to read a little more election news. In glancing over the pages I got quite interested in a Wootten Bassett Divorce Case; the burning down of Swindon station etc..

I hope soon to get my letters so as to know how business and everything else is progressing. I hope the new shop is keeping up to the mark and that the two shop girls are giving satisfaction. Have they been worrying for a 'rise' like the others?

As soon as Colley gets back from Vancouver I expect Stansfield will be asked to resign, and if he doesn't he will get kicked out. Of course I shall not support such a course, after the way I was unanimously elected a member, but really I think it is the only way in which to preserve the party. We all get on first class together and all want to stick together, except him. Things have reached a crisis and in a few days I expect he will have to take his share and go. I shall be sorry for him, but he has deliberately brought it on himself by gross mismanagement.

The further inland we get the dearer the provisions become. For instance, four and a half miles this side of the summit a small loaf costs 25 cents, whilst at the summit a cup of coffee and three slices of bread and butter costs 50 cents. But at the summit we reach the dear old Union Jack and are on British soil again and consequently can open our provisions and bake our own bread.

I don't care for Americans, but Canadians are good fellows.

I saw two wolves a few nights ago. I won't go out without my revolver again. I might easily have got at least one nice skin.

Now with fond love all round –

Your affectionate son,

Will

Sunday 1st May 1898

Mouth of White Pass, Alaska.

My dear Lill and Flo

At last we bid goodbye to Alaska. Swann and I take over the last load this evening, and tonight all our party will be sleeping under the British flag once more. We shall make the summit about midnight and just unload the donkeys, wrap ourselves in our blankets etc. and sleep out in the open on the snow as it will be too late to erect a tent and I expect we shall be far too tired.

I am still looking for Colley's return, so that I may get news of you all.

We got away from Skagway on Thursday and it is such a wicked place that I was not sorry to bid it adieu. Up here amongst the mountains it is grand; the snow is still very very deep and only on Friday last we had a fall of snow about a foot deep. But today, 1st of May, is a grand specimen of summer. So warm and fresh that I actually was forced to sing "Hail all hail, the merry month of May".

I have had an easy time today, being cook, and as there is only Swann and myself to cook for it is not an arduous task. The river here is full of dead horses so I obtain all our water for drinking purposes by melting snow. I made some nice pancakes this morning. They did well to eat with our bacon as a substitute for bread which costs 25 cents a loaf here.

Did I ever mention that I had sent a box of collars, thin underwear and various odds and ends to Vancouver to await my return. They are in charge of the Company's agent, a Mr Woods. I did not send my overcoat back, but cut off a about a foot from the bottom. My word what a task I had to hem round the bottom! I am glad I brought it on as it comes in very useful, and is not at all awkward now cut down.

The time is slipping on quickly, and now we have crossed the mountains and are practically down to the lakes; we shall slip along quickly too. We shall make a way towards Teslyn. Shall strike the Hootalingua River and probably a part of us will go to Teslyn and the others down the river towards the Big Salmon.

Is Mother and Father well? I hope you keep them from worrying. Don't do too much yourselves and, for sure, don't let them overdo it.

And now, dear kiddies, believe me, your affectionate brother,
Will

Friday 20th May 1898

Log Cabin
7 miles from Lake Bennett,
NWT Canada

Dear Father and Mother,

I have lots of things to tell you, but in telling one half I shall doubtless forget the other. And, indeed, I am feeling far more ready to receive letters than to write them, for my last letter from home was written by Lill and dated 10th March.

Colley has not turned up yet with the mail bag and we fear he must be ill for he is weeks overdue. Nothing would be more acceptable just now than a letter, not even a nugget. Patience is a fine thing, but as difficult to possess as, say 'letters'. To a donkey driver especially, patience is an extremely difficult virtue to cultivate. True, Job was a man of patience, and Job kept a good many donkeys, but he didn't look after them himself, or he would have lost his character: we read that 'his servants' came and told him when disaster overtook his mokes, so he evidently was not looking after them himself. Lucky Job. Often I've wished our 'jacks' in the hands of Sabeans. I have had a week at cooking for the whole party for a change, but am back with the donkeys again now. Of the two I like the latter work although it is more conducive to profanity, but we shall be at Bennett in a fortnight and then shall all get an easy time whilst waiting for the ice to break up on the lakes. This will probably be in about a month or five weeks. Then we shall embark and four days sailing will take us to the Big Salmon River where we are in the centre of the Gold country. Such is our present programme.

We lost another donkey last week, so our present number is reduced to four. The season for dogs is over, the ice and snow being too rotten for sleighing. The roads, or trails, for they cannot be called roads, are in an awful condition. The sun during the day is very hot, so that the snows melt very rapidly and the trails are all under water. Sometimes it is over a donkey's head. Often we have to haul them out with ropes to prevent them drowning. Horses are no good at all, as they refuse the work. Sacrifice of horses this past winter and spring is awful. For the 40 miles from Skagway to Bennett it works out to a horse for every 15 yards. The horses are bought for something like 10 or 12 for 150 dollars. They carry 250 lbs which at 15 cents a lb. makes them more than pay for themselves in one trip. Hence horses are little thought of. Often the trail is so bad that it takes a day to go three miles. Today for instance it will be very bad, for during the night it has been snowing and the bad places will be just covered up. There are places where by putting the foot down in a certain spot you may cross safely, whilst an inch either to right or left will land you into 5 or 6 feet of soft slimy mud from which it is impossible to extricate oneself without help. Of course we never go alone. I have Williams with me today. It is marvellous how cleverly the donkeys pick their way, but often the treacherous ground lands them into dangerous mud or water holes and causes much hard work and un-parliamentary language.

We are still high up amongst the mountains and camped in the heart of a pine forest in a very healthy situation.

My health is grand and my appetite is enormous, so it will be an expensive affair when I come home to board.

We are getting on much better together now. Stansfield has been brought to his senses somewhat and Young has withdrawn from the party. Whether or not Stansfield retains leadership will depend upon his conduct during the next few weeks.

We shall build a raft at Bennett for the baggage, provisions etc, or perhaps a boat.

Friday 20th Evening

Dear Mammie and Dad,

Since writing this morning, we have had news from Colley. He is laid up at Skagway with a sprained ankle so we shall soon have your letters now as one of us will go back to fetch the mail. Hurrah! Am sorry for Colley though. Stansfield has just come in with the information that he is going to Bennett in an hour and as there is a post office there I shall finish this and give it him to post. We have just learnt that there is a mail at Bennett twice a week and as it will perhaps be six weeks before we leave there, will you please write by return of post and address to W T White, Southport Yukon Syndicate Limited, (S.Y.S. Party) Post Office, Lake Bennett, British Columbia, via New York.

I must get it before we leave, and in any case it would follow me within a week or so to Walsh City. You may write once a week to the address at Bennett until I give you another address, but no more to Teslyn as we shall be unable to fetch them so easily.

Walsh City is at the mouth of the Big Salmon and the NWMP have established a depot there, so that I can easily get things sent on from Bennett. Oh it will be good to get news from you.

It seems strange that June is near for we have snow all around us still. All our drinking water is got from melting snow. We dare not touch the streams; there are so many putrifying horses lying about.

We had a bad time today with the donkeys. They were down several times and one of them we nearly lost entirely. It fell into a mud hole until only its neck and head remained above; it was tough work getting him out I can assure you. Several times I was waist deep myself. You mustn't worry about me though for I have rubbers up to the waist. Still sometimes the water runs in over the top and then you feel inclined to say ----, still if you don't say it, it's alright.

Seriously though we are all very careful indeed in this respect. We always wear two pairs of stockings at one time and the moment we get in, we change our two pairs of wet ones for dry ones. Sometimes we change two and even three times a day. We never go out without a dry pair of thick woollen stockings in our pocket, in case of need. The feet are a very important item here.

We came across the track of a bear in the woods last night. Wilson is out trying to shoot it.

Well I must dry up now. Next time I write I hope I shall be able to say I have had your letters.

Your affectionate son,
Will

28 May 1898

Forest Camp,
Nr. Log Cabin, near Lake Bennett.

My dear Lill

I will write to you this time because you understand the troubles of a cook. I am cooking again this week, and at the present moment am supposed to be cooking bacon and beans though in reality it is the heat from the fire that cooks them. Still that's nothing to do with it, so I'll resume - when I've given those peaches a stir, for today I'm stewing some peaches for the second course. I think the cooking talent must be hereditary for I have not killed anyone yet – hard as I've tried. Besides bacon and beans for dinner, I have given them as follows on various occasions: treacle pudding, jam roly poly, baked rice pudding and jam, apple dumplings, stewed apricots, peaches, prunes and figs, raisin pudding, etc. etc. etc. Then in the morning I always boil porridge and fry bacon. With the bacon we eat 'slap jacks' which are warranted to give anyone indigestion within five minutes. i.e. if I cook them. You might send me a few recipes. We have not things to cook like you have – only necessaries, so don't go in for anything grand. I bake bread each day and often a few raisin buns. Oh! I should like you to see this boy. What a saving I shall be for Nellie. She won't need to keep a cook – the cook will keep her and she shall be parlour maid and having nothing to do with the kitchen.

Next week it's my turn off with the donkeys. Swann, Williams and I will be by ourselves as the others are off in another direction moving the boats towards the lake.

I am enjoying life pretty considerably and should be happy if only I could get to hear how you are at home and how Nellie is.

Colley returned with the news that our letters had all gone to Teslyn before he got to Vancouver and that the postman capsized his boat on the Stikine and lost all the letters. So you must please rewrite all letters from 10th March to, say, middle of April and address everything in future to me at Lake Bennett.

Life here is very free and easy and if only a letter came occasionally I should be finding it quite A1. Our dress out here in the forest and lonely places is remarkable for its freedom. It is very hot at times, 90° in the sun, and a good plunge into the streams is grand. It is after nine o'clock in the evening and the sun is not down yet. It is up about half past one in the morning; practically it is never dark at all now.

We are working so hard since we crossed the White Pass, and we generally manage to find time to wash our faces once a week whether we need it or not.

It was a lucky thing I got attached to such a good party for I am just in my element. Swann is a retired farmer of Southport, age about 55 or 60 but tough as steel. He is a Wesleyan and knows our great men of the north, such as Charles Garrett. Williams is a married man about 30. When he left England he was superintendent of a large Methodist Sunday School and has a lovely gold watch chain which his church gave him on leaving.

Be sure you look after Nellie, Lill. Get her to come to Bridport as much as you possibly can. I don't want her to go out to business again if it can be avoided for she really cannot stand it, but if she is staying at home for any length of time it will make her miserable and then she will be wanting to get out again. I do feel anxious about her but leave you to do all you can to cheer her up till the prodigal returns. Tell her and Mother that it won't be long now, as you can get to the Yukon in much less than a week when the ice breaks.

And now I must close as sleep calls. I don't know whether I shall add to this ere I get an opportunity of posting so will say night nightie. Take care of yourselves and steer clear of all illness. With love to self and all, from

Will.

I believe the Southport Guardian publishes news of the party from time to time. You might send to them for back numbers with matters relating to us and get them to send on to you a copy when anything fresh appears.

Sunday 5th June 1898
Lake Bennett, B.C.

Dear Father and Mother,

This morning Williams, Swann and I had a little service to ourselves. We sang some of Sankey's hymns and Williams read us a chapter. I wanted him to select 137th Psalms, but he preferred and read 40th Isaiah, especially the last four verses for we have all had a very rough and tiresome journey, but thank goodness we are practically through to Bennett at last, after 10 weeks of weary toil.

At last! This is not a shout of joy on turning out my first nugget, but merely a sigh of relief on arriving at the limpid waters of Bennett; the headwaters of the mighty Golden Yukon. Skagway, only 33 miles away. We left during the first week in April and after ten weeks of incessant toil, you can imagine, far better than I could describe, the refreshing sight we experienced when, tired and travel-stained, we turned a spur of the mountains and saw Lake Bennett nestling almost at our feet. Bennett City is the starting point for pilgrims to Dawson, and at present it comprises hundreds of tents of various sorts and two or three log cabins. In a fortnight or three weeks, this city will probably cease to exist as everyone will have finished boat building and started on the voyage down stream.

The trail across the White Pass is not so difficult as one would expect. Of course it means an awful amount of hard work and takes quite a time to accomplish, but in no sense does it present any features of danger or any obstacle that could reasonably discourage one. The trail is unquestionably very bad but then that is only what we were led to expect. I have driven our donkeys over every inch of the road and had some exciting times, but more of that anon. The most objectionable feature of the trail at the present time is the large number of putrid horses which line every few yards of the way. Over 3500 carcasses in every stage of decomposition are on the track from Skagway to Bennett and the stench is – well I won't swear! Ugh!! Shall I ever be able to eat roast beef again, without smelling rotten horse? But worst of all, perhaps, are the mosquitoes. They are awful. One has no peace, day or night. We have just lit a moss fire in order to suffocate them, but only succeeded in nearly choking ourselves. I am simply covered about the face, neck, arms and hands with bumps which resemble a bad attack of 'stinging nettles'. And also, one night, whilst sleeping out in the open, I kicked my blanket off and the diabolical fiends got at my feet awful, so that they resemble a piece of patchwork, being covered with red and white patches.

"They get in your coffee, they get in your tea;
They never leave you one moment free.
They jump on the butter, they swim in the jam;
And they swarm in your mouth if you dare to say 'damn'"
(There! We now have two poets in the family).

Sunday 12th June

Lake Bennett, B.C.

Dear Father and Mother,

I'm a nice comfortable sight at this moment and heartily wish I could get my photo taken. I have headed my letter 'Bennett' but as a matter of fact I am at our old spot eight miles off. It is Sunday, our day of rest, and I was off this morning to pay a visit to Williams and Swann. I got here about nine o'clock, in time for breakfast, and now am lounging with only my shirt and pants on, trying my best to keep my temper and write you a few lines. But it is hard work for the sun is almost tropical and the mosquitoes are – oh may I be preserved from using bad language.

Stansfield and I have been very busy this past week for we have opened a shop in Bennett. We have been unfortunate enough to lose about 1200 lbs of provisions and as we have no more ready money within immediate reach, we are raising the necessary funds to replace the loss by selling some of the articles we were taking to trade with the Indians. Lake Bennett is very busy and we took over 200 dollars last week which has quite set us up again, and we shall now commence boat building.

It is so hot now that I sleep out of doors every night. It is far more pleasant and healthier.

Sunday 19th June 1898

I had a most interesting experience last week. One night or rather morning, it was about 2 o'clock, I was awakened by an agitated female clasping my feet with all her might and sighing "Oh mister, Oh mister. What shall I do?" Naturally, I suggested that she might let go my feet as a start. I was sleeping at one of our caches about four miles out from Bennett and was quite alone, so you can imagine how I felt. But (to my sorrow shall I say) I soon discovered that this was no 'Potiphar's wife', and my heroic dream of playing 'Joseph' was not likely to come off. It seems the real reason for all this agitation arose from the fact that whilst this fair damsel was journeying to Bennett in the cool of the morning, about 100 yards from where I was sleeping she came face to face with a huge bear which very rudely stood on its hind legs and placed its two front paws to its nose. This was more than poor feminine nerves could stand. She fled to a pile of goods near, in order to hide, and there discovered me sleeping on the ground and so hailed me as her saviour.

I made her sit down a while and offered to walk along the road with her and in time she got calmed and soothed, just as the ladies do when ministered to by the gender masculine. (We have some funny sights and experiences out here) I saw no trace of the bear, but no doubt she saw one; they are by no means rare in this locality and at night come down on the trail, attracted perhaps by the dead horses.

If you care, you can insert the above letter in the "Bridport News". I should like friends to see that 'the very last chap in the world whom they thought would go to Klondyke is well and hearty.

During this past week matters have come to a crisis, resulting in the resignation and withdrawal of Messrs, Colley, Wilson, Norris and Porter. Consequently, the SYS now consists of Messrs. Stansfield, Swann, Williams and White. This is a good thing for us as the results will not have to be divided amongst so many. The other members were nice fellows but very lazy and we are far better off without them. Stansfield is not all that he ought to be but Swann, Williams and myself get on splendid together and keep a sharp look out. This withdrawal reduces the assets of the Company by half but this is immaterial since the difficult portion of the journey is over.

By next Sunday (26th) we shall be sailing down the river towards the Hootalingua which we shall probably reach on the 28th and then, hurrah for gold hunting.

Our outfit will be considerable. We shall have one canoe the 'Lily Harold' to carry 1000 lbs and one person. One scow to carry the donkeys and dogs and one boat to carry 4 or 5 tons. I shall probably be in charge of the canoe, Williams the 'Noah's Ark', and Stansfield and Swann the boat. My interest in the concern is £70 out of a total of £670 but if I can see a chance of bettering myself I can withdraw at any time. One of us will be in England before Christmas if we can strike a good claim. The one will probably be Stansfield as he is going to get the thing floated as a company to raise say £50,000 capital and take over our claim. Very nice if it comes off!

I am going to church this evening with Williams. Church is conducted in a canvas tent. I don't know what sect is in possession.

I do wish I could only get a letter from someone. We shall be away from here before the mail comes and I am directing all letters to be sent on to Hootalingua.

Meanwhile, will you please put me up a little box for Christmas. Mother can put me in one of her Christmas puddings, only it must be a very small one as the package had better not weigh more than 10 lbs. Please wrap everything in newspaper so that there will be something to read. I don't know that I am in want of anything, except perhaps a kiss from you now and then. It seems such a long, long time since I heard from anyone. Just fancy March 10th since I heard. The box I have asked you to send had better be addressed to me at Dawson City.

Stansfield and I will probably take a pleasure trip down to Dawson. At any rate one of us will go as it is only a few hundred miles from where we shall be. Of course, it won't be till the cold weather comes, but all newspapers sent there will reach me sometime or other.

And now I will turn in. It is light here; sun has just gone down, 10.30. Will be up again about 1.

5

SUMMER AT THE N.W.M.P POST LAKE TAGISH, AND A CHANGE OF PLAN

Early July
NWMP Post
Tagish

My own dear Dad and Mammy,

Hurrah! I have a 1/4 hour in which to write and tell you of my thrilling experience since leaving Bennett.

The day after leaving Bennett a big storm came up and we were near 'kingdom come.' As it was we got blown on to a rocky shore and got on the rocks. After working up to our waists amongst the waves we managed to get the boat off and round a point into a sheltered bay where we found we had sprung a leak. We beached the boat and spent two days in repairing her, after which we continued our journey and after various stormy experiences arrived here at the Police Camp, a haven of rest for us. When getting the boat off the rocks, I was washed off my feet. Fortunately Stansfield was in the boat and managed to catch me and haul me in. These lakes are very large and much like the sea in many places.

Our plans are likely to be altered again in consequence of news we have heard here. We may go down to Atlin Lake between here and Teslyn. If so, we may be able to have a wash up this winter. Anyway, we shall be near and able to get to England in a month at any time of the year. If we strike anything rich, you can bet your bottom dollar I shall soon hop across to see you all. Wish I could only strike a letter from you. I cannot say just yet whether we shall strike Atlin Lake or not, so you need not alter the postal arrangements made at Bennett when last I wrote you - sometime last week I think.

'Sandy Bay', where we repaired our boat, was the loveliest little place I was ever in. We had it entirely to ourselves and named it. We had some grand fishing, pulling out trout about 5 lbs. in weight is grand business and first class when it gets to eating.

And now I must say goodbye again for we are just off.
With love to all,
Will

16th July 1898
NWMP Post
Lake Tagish NWT

My dear Lill,
My last letter is dated 12th inst.

I am going across to the police camp the other side of the creek, with a few letters, so am sending one of my own at the same time.

Stansfield and Williams left about three o'clock this morning for Atlin Lake on a placer prospecting tour. I am left behind in order to do a bit of likely quartz prospecting about six miles off, after which I shall go across and join them. It will most likely take me two or three days before I shall be ready to leave here. It has come on to rain so I am not starting just yet. There is an Indian village just across the lake and you would enjoy a visit amongst the squaws I am sure. They are quite friendly and have shown their neighbourly feeling by taking possession of our fishing net without so much as a 'by-your-leave'. At Tagish Post I saw four Indians of another tribe all heavily manacled and chained together. They will most likely be shot for murdering a Klondyke miner and wounding another. They seemed quite unconcerned.

The fishing here is just grand. My word, I should like you, Mater and Dad, to have such feeds as we are having. There are scarcely

Broadway, Skagway, Alaska. May 1898
F H NOWELL / THE ANCHORAGE MUSEUM OF HISTORY OF ART, ALASKA

Prospectors camp at Lake Bennett 1898   E A HEGG COLL / YUKON ARCHIVES

Lake Tagish 1898   RCMP

Tagish Post 1897-1900   RCMP
Headquarters of 'H' Division (Southern Yukon)

any small fish. They average from 4 to 7 lbs each and by putting the net down overnight, one is sure of getting from 30 to 100 trout and white fish about this size. The flesh is as tender and tasty as anything I ever tasted and bones are so large as to cause no trouble at all.

The country is looking grand just now. The wild flowers are more varied and more beautiful than we find in Britain. Spring onions or chipples grow here in abundance and are a great convenience for seasoning.

We are all very hopeful about the success of the party in this neighbourhood.

Instead of sending letters to Fort Selkirk, please address them to Lake Tagish and then if we move from here they can be sent on to us. In another three months I shall be able to get from here to Skagway in two days by means of steamer and railroad, so I hope we strike something that will be worth stopping for.

I am getting quite a barbarian. Had you met me in the woods this morning before the rain came on, you would have found me clothed simply in my woollen vest and pants. I guess I shall leave off the pants next. At any rate I must leave off this gossiping and paddle my canoe across to the post.

With love to yourself and all,
Your affectionate brother,
Will
Wish Harold many happy returns of the day.

My dear Daddy

I am just commencing to wish you "Many happy returns of the Day" for although it is still July I don't expect this will reach you before 21st September.

We are here in a very strange position. On my last letter I think I told you Stansfield and Williams had gone off to Atlin and that I was following in a day or two. About the middle of the week Williams came back - dead beat and quite exhausted. He said that they had missed the trail and got lost in the forests and that in consequence of heavy rains and numbers of bear, he had had only seven hours sleep out of seventy seven. Stansfield was too done up to return but was going to have a good rest and then try and reach the Lake. He had four days provisions left and Williams and I were to secure an Indian guide and take over a month's provisions with the donkeys, and meet him on the shores of the lake. I may add that in order to make four days provisions, Stansfield had to shoot one of the dogs and, according to his arrangements, we were to try and reach him before the 4th day to prevent him eating dog flesh. We secured an Indian for a suit of overalls and a piece of showy cloth and he landed us here two days ago, but - no signs of Stansfield. Jack Williams and a friend who has come with us, spent yesterday searching the woods but no sign of life anywhere.

Today, they have gone inland to try and find him. If they do not succeed, I shall be inclined to think Master Bruin knows something about the matter for he is very numerous around here. He showed himself to the donkeys the other night and so scared them that they don't want to leave the camp fire after dark. You can be quite sure I don't stir many yards without my revolver. I am in charge of camp today so am taking things pretty easy - storing up energy for digging. Very few white men have ever been on this lake, probably not more than a dozen, but the Indians tell us there is a large party about 20 miles off which may or may not be true.

2 day's later

Dear Dad,

Williams and I rescued Stansfield yesterday. He had got into an almost inaccessible valley and there had the misfortune to tread with his bare feet upon some hot ashes. He had shot some birds and was not doing badly. You can imagine what we had to come through when it took us two hours to cut through less than a quarter of a mile of forest. Williams and I wielded our axes unceasingly and weren't we glad to get at our canteen tins well supplied with the juice of stewed apples. Stansfield's foot is bad, but he is doctoring it well and in a few days we hope he will be about as usual.

Tell Bert this is a grand country for feeding. We had a duck for supper last night and today for dinner we had stewed squirrel and beans, roast duck and green peas; rice and stewed raisins. This is quite like the papers pictured it isn't it? But the mosquitoes are - but no, I'll leave that subject for it'll only end by my swearing and Jack Williams strongly objects to my indulging in that kind of thing. He has promised to occupy the pulpit some Sunday at Bridport so I hope you will some day have the pleasure of knowing him. His friendship and society are invaluable to me for we can meet on common ground. We both love the Old Book and its teachings, although our opinions are not always in harmony. Many and vigorous are the arguments we have on eternal punishment, transmigration of souls, temperance, theatres, etc. Jack is a terror at debating. Actually replied to one of my arguments by informing me that it was the Devil's Soothing Syrup.

We like the look of Atlin immensely and are very sanguine of success here.

About 20th July

Dear Dad,

I have just come across from Atlin Lake to Tagish, about 10 miles, in order to see whether there are any letters for us. You can imagine how anxious I am to get one. I trust I may. I shall have to paddle the canoe about three miles up the lake to reach the post. Some of the police are English and get the papers so I am well stocked with Tit Bits, Standard, Liverpool Daily Post, New York Herald etc. Most of these dated between 21st May and 7th June.

We found a very good specimen of gold yesterday and if we can only trace it to its source we should get a Bonanza. Anyway it is encouraging and shows that we are all amongst it.

And now I must finish as I have a lot to do if I am to reach Atlin before dark. I will mention on the envelope whether or not I found a letter waiting for me.

With fondest love all round and best wishes for "many happy returns of the day"

Your affectionate son, Will.

Sure you let Nellie see.

August 12th or 13th
Lake Tagish
N.W.M. Police Camp

My dear Mother and sisters,

I cannot keep it in! Good news will keep they say, but I cannot keep it, so here goes!!! I have been in a gold rush; passed through many privations and adventures in getting to the diggings; seen nuggets dug out of the ground and staked out two claims. The surface indications are good but there was no time to test further, owing to lack of provisions as you will see. That is the whole matter in a nutshell, so now for detail.

I am not sure whether I mentioned in my last letter that we were leaving our camp here and taking a few weeks' provisions and prospecting round Lake Atlin. This program was commenced but owing to a lucky accident Stansfield got lost and the outfit had to return here to replenish and prepare for another start. This proved a lucky matter for us for before we left a man came down from the mountains to the Police Post to say that he had found a big gold bearing district about 70 miles off. This you will no doubt have heard of under the names, Pine Creek or Lake Atlin. Capt. Strickland, the commanding officer at once started off with five of his men, and we hustled back to camp and hurriedly packed a few things together. Capt. Strickland had gone by way of Taku Arm, but acting on the advice of an Indian we went across the Atlin Lake about 8 miles, from whence we expected to reach the diggings in about 15 miles, thus being the first in the field. But alas! What we thought was Atlin proved to be a nameless piece of water about 12 miles long, and when we got to the end of it we were in reality about 60 miles from Pine Creek. Had we known this our hearts would surely have failed us but happily we were in ignorance. The only outlet proved to be a small swift stream and this we concluded must eventually reach the real Atlin. It did - eventually. It was very rapid and about 10 miles in length, but it took us 2 days and a half to negotiate this distance in the canoe. Never before had men been down that river. Every few hundred yards we found the drift wood of ages stretching until

"Like a dam the mighty wreck
Lay right athwart the stream".

As much as fifteen tons of timber would be collected in some of these piles. At such places we would unload and do a portage. At other times we would spend many hours in cutting and hacking our way through. When at last we did reach Atlin, all hopes of our being first in the field had vanished. For two days we pulled down the lake against head winds and then the water threatening to swamp us, we had to land on an island. For 30 hours we lay there storm bound, the rollers outside the bay coming in as though from the Atlantic itself. We had not yet reached the diggings and knew not how far off we were, but we found our larder was in a very poor state. If we did not soon reach Pine Creek we should have to turn back or risk starvation. As it was, it was necessary to go on short rations at once. Just as we were putting out, we were overjoyed to see a small canoe in the distance and its occupants proved to be a party of the Police who had started several days after us and come the same route. But alas! these poor boys were worse off than we, for they had eaten their last meal several hours before, so our small stock of provisions had to undergo another diminution. Before nightfall however we reached Pine Creek soon enough to stake a good claim but not the first in the field by a long way. We staked out a claim, each on Pine Creek and also another on a creek adjoining where a further discovery had been made. Our provisions were now at a very low ebb, so we started off back again without much testing, but the discovery claim is turning out gold in large quantities and of the very finest quality. It did one's eyesight good to watch it. I called my first claim "Bridport Placer Claim". It took us longer to get home than we expected and we looked a bit blue yesterday morning when we ate our last meagre meal at 4 o'clock, and were yet far from camp. But luckily a grand breeze sprung up and the canoe fairly plunged through the water, so that in a few hours we had gone as far as we previously went in a few days. Sometime during the afternoon we arrived at the police camp and there the boys were very kind and cooked us such a meal as we hadn't tasted for weeks. Bacon, potatoes, beans, stewed prunes, bread and butter, and coffee ad. lib. Oh! my word, you ought to have seen those things disappear. It takes a week on short rations to whet your appetite. And now we are having a day's rest after so much fatigue, and I can assure you it is appreciated by W.T.W. Not that I am in any way knocked up. Was never better in my life. This open air knocking about is the making of me. I am actually fatter and heavier than when I left England whilst my face would put a tomato in the shade.

We are in for a real good thing at Pine Creek. I expect to make several hundred pounds out of it before Spring. We shall buy as many claims as possible and then a company will be formed to work the lot. I expect Stansfield will leave Williams or me in charge and get off to London in a few weeks. Capt.Cartright, son of Sir Richard Cartright, has the claim next to Bridport Mine, so you see I am in aristocratic surroundings.

All letters, papers, parcels, etc. can now be sent to Tagish as we shall be here all the winter. You cannot imagine how awfully anxious I am for news. Things are so stirring up here that one gets little time for thinking, or I should go out of my mind imagining all sorts of catastrophies. But I am trusting in one above and trying to be patient, fearing no evil amongst those I love.

And now I'm going to have a bathe, so ta-ra-ra-.

I am expecting to hear all sorts of news when the mail arrives. Bert will, no doubt, be married and living a quiet sedate life. Flo will be composing poetry still. Harold, doubtless, will be attending to the wants of half a dozen Phyllises, and Lil will be worried out of her life to keep the lot of you in decent trim till her big brother gets back to relieve her next year. Ah well – give 'em all my love and put a halfpenny in their stockings at Christmas with my best wishes. I hope to hear the new shop has proved a good venture and been a Klondyke in itself. I do hope Dad is having a good season and that he is a little more docile now. Tell him to put himself under your care till I get back and then I'll take him in charge myself for I am convinced he needs lots of looking after. As for you, Mother dear, I can only ask you to take all the care you can. Father and the girls I know will look after you well, but like Dad, you want to be nursed sometimes. Do be careful this Winter, both of you. Just think how I should feel when I got back if anything had happened to you meanwhile. What would my success be worth then ?

Adieu fond love from
Will

Somewhere about 9th September 1898
N.W.M. Police Camp

Dear Everyone

I have just come seventy miles in a canoe for letters and all the way from Pine Creek, and the first man I met when I landed here was Segt. Major Iles who said, "Well I'm d-----. I've just sent your letters up to Pine Creek on the steamer. They were brought to Tagish by the captain of the steamboat this morning ."

Such is my luck, but I shall start back again in the morning. With a good breeze I shall get back in a day. Tonight I am sleeping at the camp with the police. They are fine fellows and have been a great help to us. We are known to them all and wherever we go are always sure of a welcome. We were able to help three of them with food on one occasion when they were 80 miles from camp, and about three weeks ago Stansfield was fortunate enough to save one of them from drowning. I was with Stansfield at the time. It was dusk and we were on a lonely sheet of water when we heard cries and moans that went through us almost. We found a poor fellow had capsized and was seized with a kind of cramp: we were able to reach him in time to save him. So now we feel quite at home when near a Police Camp.

Pine Creek is going to turn out well from all accounts, but as it cannot be worked during the winter we shall not stay there more than a few weeks just to give it a thorough testing. So that the time may not be wasted, we are going to the island at the foot of Marsh Lake, about 25 miles from here, and there we shall build a large cabin and use it as a restaurant, and shall probably make many thousands of dollars. Meals will be at least a dollar each and probably half as much again. As soon as the ice comes, probably 5,000 to 10,000 people will come out of the country, and these we hope to be our customers.

It is just a speculation and we cannot lose by it; then again, it will give us something to do during the long winter. We are making preparations to receive the ice. It is glorious weather so far, not at all too cold for sleeping in the open air. In fact I nearly always sleep in the open. We expect the ice in about three weeks or a month probably or it may hold off as late as November 1st, but not later.

Well, I am pretty tired now and will not stay to write more or ask any questions.

Give my love to all. I am praying my letters will be full of good news from all quarters.

With best love, Will

6

MOVE TO ATLIN AND PREPARATIONS FOR WINTER

23rd September 1898
Atlin City

Dear Dad,

At last! After seven months and a week!!! Your birthday, 21st September 1898 will long be a red letter day with me, for on this date I received two letters, the first since leaving Vancouver. One was from Nellie dated 7th July and the other from Lill dated 5th August, so you see there is quite a big mail for me somewhere. I expect I shall get them dribbling in slowly now, hope so at any rate. It was the greatest wonder in the world they reached me though. I went to Tagish for letters (about 80 miles) and they said they had sent them up. When I got to the landing here there was a steamer just about to go. I hurriedly wrote a few lines and gave to a chap to post and then saw a policeman I knew. He was just off back by the steamer, having been unable to find me. Had I missed him my letters would have returned to Tagish.

I am just off with Stansfield to a big discovery in the northwest and I intend to locate a claim in the name of yourself, provided it is good. If I can secure it in some way and it is a good one, it would be worth coming to claim. But that is to be seen. This discovery is about sixty miles away under an active volcano with a glacier on it. The mountains are all covered with a beautiful fresh white sheet of snow, but we have had none so low as this yet. We are 2500 feet above sea level here and about 120 miles from the White Pass.

I had expected writing a big letter this time, but must commence to pack things together for our expedition to the North West. There is also a steamer in and I want to get someone to carry this to Skagway and post it for me. So I must dry up and write a longer dose next time.

Williams and I are going to start a Bible Class here on Sunday afternoons amongst the miners, so you see my heart is still pointing in the right direction. I will send a description of our first meeting to the Methodist Times.

With very fondest love to all,
Your affectionate son
Will

P.S. I saw two fine big nuggets this morning - one 42 dollars, 30 cents and the other 25 dollars, 45 cents. They were dug out two or three days ago.

Sunday 9th October 1898

Atlin City
British Columbia

My dear Father & Mother

Ever since leaving Bennett last June we have had a young Scotch midshipman travelling with us, but he is now about to leave us and return to Glasgow so as to be home for Christmas. (Lucky fellow, how I envy him that privilege!)

He is a frank happy lad of nineteen and has been the great fun maker of our party, so we are sorry to lose him. His name is David Kirkwood and should he ever chance to come to Bridport I have told him you would be pleased to put him up for a day or two. He is taking this letter with him so I am pretty sure it will reach you, if posted in Vancouver.

I have some big news for you this time. You will be surprised to hear that I have resigned from the S.Y.S. - Stansfield's Yukon Swindle as we have christened it. Yes, his mad schemes and actions make matters unbearable and greatly to his astonishment I handed in my resignation on the 4th. This act had the effect of upsetting the whole company for on the following day Williams withdrew and entered into partnership with me, and yesterday Swann resigned and is going to work by himself. Thus Stansfield is now the remains of the great S.Y.S. party I met on board the Lake Heron eight months ago. We are expecting some little trouble in dividing up the assets, but beyond the unpleasantness of rows we shall get all that belongs to us.

The miners here are a decent set of men. Stansfield is known and detested; Williams and I are also known, but from appearances scarcely 'detested' yet, and we have been told by some of the most influencial miners in the camp that if there is any bother they will call a miners' meeting and superintend the division of goods themselves, so you see we are on the sunny side of the street. Of course, we shall now each have our own mines and as we have reason to believe them good, things are very rosy. There was another discovery on my birthday, and W. and I were both able to locate claims, so I am now the possessor of three mines and W. and I have bought a 4/5th interest in two others. Of course, we cannot work them during the winter; some we shall most likely sell in the Spring when the rush comes in and demand is brisk. Everyone expects far greater discoveries than any hitherto made, as old-timers say it is the best looking country for prospecting they have ever seen. Meanwhile, there is the Winter to face, and W & I are both in for making money. We have secured a lovely corner plot of ground on the principal street (Rant Avenue) here in the City, and have commenced to build our log cabin on it. The plot is 100 feet, facing the Avenue, and 50 feet deep and is a corner lot which will no doubt fetch a big price when the Spring rush comes. Our cabin is 17 x 12 inside and we shall build it high enough to allow a sort of primitive attic to store our goods in.

We have several projects in our mind for making money, but shall most likely do a bit of everything. Money is not difficult to make here, where the smallest coin in use is equal to one shilling and a halfpenny (25 cents) and it costs us nothing to live. The days are still warm, except when the wind blows, but the nights are bitter and one feels glad of one's fur robe to sleep in. We shall hurry on with our house as the tent is getting cold for sleeping in, although one night last week I had to sleep out on the shores of a Lake sixteen miles away and the frost was so keen that it covered the water with ice an inch thick. Fortunately, I had my bedding with me in case I was overtaken by the dark. I was alone but made a big fire and slept as close to it as I dare. But even then, you can guess it must have been cold for my waterproof ground sheet which I had pulled over my head was covered with a thin coating of ice where my breath had frozen. But I like this outside life after all. There is something so fresh and exhilarating about it.

I made a big fire in our stove this morning and had a warm bath in the tent. Some woman passed and glanced down a hole in the roof, but like the priest and the Levite she passed on the other side. One gets used to this kind of treatment out here.

Of course, Mother, I have been wearing my thick underwear for sometime, but I have never worn my woollen top shirts until today. They fit me first class and feel "bootifool". I am wearing them with my jacket off just to show them off.

I thought of you all on the 6th eating my birthday pudding. Kirkwood made us what he called a dumpling pudding - fearfully and wonderfully made with ginger sauce to match, so you see I didn't altogether go puddingless. That last word so tickled me that I inadvertently put the heel of my boot in the ink, but fortunately have not spilt it all. I made nearly half-a-pint this morning, from some ink powder.

I am hoping soon to send you some photos of the locality, also of this individual. We are getting Kirkwood to buy a Kodak in Vancouver and send us up the printing out paper and so on. We shall be able to do a big business here this Winter at a dollar a photo, I hope.

Williams and I have known each other now ever since we left England and thoroughly trust each other, so it is something to be thankful for, isn't it? We both mean work, but not Sunday work. Sunday is a day that is never observed in this country. Everyone works just the same as on other days, but here in Atlin we hope to try and set a better example and get a little chapel going.

The 6th October was the first day that skating was possible but there is a little warm spell on for the last two days. I was able to buy a splendid 2 guinea pair of Acme skates last Summer, and hope to lend them out at two and a half dollars per day for 'gents wishing sport'. As they only cost me 5 dollars, they will soon bring in money. Nearly everyone seems to have forgotten their skates. In the division W & I shall get a donkey, a team of dogs for sleighing, and a couple of boats, I suppose, and the donkey and dogs ought to earn lots of money. So you see, two saving boys like us, will soon get to Klondyke one way or another.

And now it is getting too dark to write (5 o'clock) so I will see about some supper. The big meal of the day with us.

So bye-bye for a time xxxxxxxxxxx Will

11th October 1898

Atlin City

My dear brothers and sisters,

It's Bridport Fair today I expect so I will send you a few lines as a "fairing" although it will be a good month before you get it, I expect. My fairing comes tomorrow. I am longing for breakfast to come. I don't think I shall be able to sleep tonight but, if I do, it will be only to dream of mutton chops. We so seldom get fresh meat that when we do we have to chalk it up as a red letter day. By fresh meat I don't mean such things as squirrel, grouse and duck. We are surfeited with these. No, I mean big meat such as we get in England. Someone shot a bear a few weeks ago, but I had to deny the pleasure of 'bear steak'. Today, however, the Indians came in from a hunt, bringing with them a carcase of a mountain goat or sheep. Although the price was 50 cents per lb. we couldn't resist the temptation and "Hurrah! Mutton chops for breakfast".

Winter is settling down upon us now. This morning the ground was white with snow again, but the sun at mid-day is still powerful and it soon melts. In a few days now, the frost will commence in earnest, and then - well, we've no pipes to burst out here, except those inside of us, and we'll do our best to keep them warm. Our cabin is nearly up. We have been delayed a little or it would have been finished by now.

I expect Bert and Harold have been down in the fair field having coker nut shies as in days of yore. I can imagine it all, although so many thousands of miles away. You girls would have a gay time if you could see me mending clothes. The holes in my stockings somehow get too big for darning and I have to patch them with pieces from the legs of old ones. Fortunately, I am well supplied in this department. Mending my trousers and shirts is awful hard lines though I generally have to shriek a dozen times before I finish, for I mistake the pincushion and stick the needle or pins into my thigh, or something else, equally painful. I am awfully obliged to you girls and Nell for my sewing bundle and its contents. Everyone admires and envies it and I am sure it is the best thing of its kind in camp. It is invaluable to me.

Bert and Harold will be pleased to hear that I am getting a crack shot with the revolver. The other Sunday there was a squirrel on the top of a tree, about 50 feet high. I didn't want to kill the little chap, but I tried to get as near as I could. I fired and master squirrel fell at my feet, and then much to my amazement he jumped up unhurt and ran back to the tree again. Poor little chap, the bullet must have passed so close to him as to knock him off his perch as it whizzed past. He was so frightened when he got back that he remained in the tree immovable for many hours and then we shot him dead out of pity.

And now out of pity for you I will cease to excite you with further details of the crimes I have committed so "olive oil".

Yours Will

30th October 1898

Atlin City

Dear Mother, Father, Nell and kiddies,

It has just struck me that you will be anxious to send me a small package of letters, papers, chocolates etc. and as Colonel Hayes is going to Vancouver to fetch his wife I am getting him to bring me in a few things I am likely to run short of. He is under fairly big obligations to Williams and I so is not likely to forget the commission. He is likely to leave Vancouver about the middle of January and hopes to come in over the ice. I have had no further letters or news from you since that one letter last month so anything addressed to -

W T White

c/o Post Office, Vancouver

To be called for by Col. Hayes of Australia

will be sure to reach me. Don't send more than once unless there is plenty of time. Hayes has had to leave very suddenly owing to the lake freezing early, so that the last steamer leaves today; otherwise he was going to bring out my Christmas letters in about a fortnight. In case I should be unable to get them out in time, let me hastily wish you all "A very very very Happy Christmas." You will all be in my thoughts, dear ones. There will be a little Christmas for -

Your loving Will

P.S. I am doing well and shall be back before Christmas '99 (D.V.) with something worth coming for! More anon - W.T.W.

12th November 1898
Atlin City , B.C.

My dear Father & Mother,

I was in hopes I should be able to get my Christmas greetings out in time for them to be seasonable, but owing to the stoppage of the steamers I am afraid that will be impossible. At present we are quite shut off from the outside world but when the ice comes communications will no doubt be resumed with greater activity than before. Both Williams and I shall go out over the ice to Skagway and spend a few days in the civilised world. What a treat it will be to see a real 'tuck shop' again. We shall bring back about six hundredweight of grub with us, so as to lose no time in the Spring. We shall be able to sleigh it over the ice with ease, and it will save us four and a half cents per lb for carriage, besides giving us a week or ten days holiday.

It is nice to be one's own master again. Living is now a pleasure, and hardship is hardship no longer, because one feels that the benefit will go to those we love instead of to a company whose reputation is anything but savoury. I did well to join it, Mother dear, and I did better still to leave it.

We have a first class little log house here - the admiration of the neighbourhood I assure you. We can take our tent and go off into the mountains to hunt or to prospect whenever we like, and when we are tired of that we can come back to camp and have a nice warm house to go to.

We have plenty of the right kind of clothes and enough to eat and to spare, so let the Winter be as severe as it like we have nought to fear from it. Our cabin is a little larger than, say, the scullery at home, i.e. 12 x 14 inside and its height is 5 and 3/4 at the eaves and 7 feet in the centre. When we have the stove going she is as warm and snug as any room you were ever in. The boys in camp think so, for they like to come in of an evening and sit around the fire smoking, discussing the life of the camp, and telling yarns under the genial influence of a nice cup of hot tea, which goes down nice in this cold climate, I can assure you.

Everyone speaks well of the country. It is grand scenery, abounds in large game, has a cold but very healthy climate and is wonderfully rich in gold. When I say rich, I don't mean there is any Klondike about it - nothing so rich as that, but on the other hand, it is very widely and evenly distributed and so affords chances which the Klondike denies.

I am enclosing a small piece of the precious metal to show you in what condition it comes from the ground; this is a very fair average specimen. Sometimes, of course, nuggets fifty times that size turn up, but these are rare and the gold scattered through the country is generally about this size. I suppose the price in question is worth not less than 1/6d. or 2/-, but I couldn't tell exactly as I haven't my gold scales with me just now. This hunting for gold becomes very fascinating, especially when one has a good claim. This, I think, I already possess but, owing to Stansfield's blundering delays, no work could be done till the season was too far advanced. I shall test it as soon as ever weather permits and get to work at the earliest opportunity. We have learnt a great deal of valuable information from an old-timer who has been staying with us for a few days, an old man with over sixty years' experience, one of the most interesting characters we have yet struck.

The cold weather and I agree remarkably well. I am sure I was never so well in my life before, and my eating capacity is simply marvellous, despite the monotony of the daily menu - beans and bacon; bacon and beans; bean soup; soupy beans; fried bacon; bacon fried and so on, and so on, and so on, with judicious quantities of stewed fruits at intervals. There is plenty of fresh meat in the camp, but we do not care to buy it as the price is to too heavy for we saving lads. There were forty oxen in here when the snow came and they had to be killed to prevent them from dying. The frost of course will keep the meat till next Spring. We may get a chunk to roast for Christmas. The English boys here speak of getting up a big Christmas party to celebrate the occasion and I rather think we shall have a good do.

However we spend it though, my heart will be at home. I have never spent Christmas away from you before and the remembrance of the happy times we have always had will make me feel just the least bit homesick I expect. But never mind, we'll all be together again before next year's Christmas is upon us, if God will be so good to me. I sincerely believe I have been enabled to get here only in answer to prayer, and if I remember all you have taught me, I believe God will grant me success and bring me back to all the loved ones next year. They have a saying here: "It's hard work serving the Lord in the backwoods".

This is very true. One misses the influence of the Sunday services and the constant society of Christians far more than can be imagined by those who have never experienced it, but I am trying with God's help to live as good a life as I can, which alas! is not saying a great deal.

This is not a lady's country tell Lill and Flo, so I'm sorry I cannot invite them here for Christmas. There are probably about twenty feminines in camp now, but there are only about three at all decent. Perhaps I judge them somewhat harshly, but I go by the costume they wear; there are only three who wear dresses, and these are three nice young wives - girls with plenty of grit but essentially womanly. The other fashion in vogue here is hateful and repulsive - when it is not too ludicrous, which is not too often.

The camp here is a wonderfully quiet one for a mining district, so you need not fear any shooting matches or fighting.

The B.C. Government are stepping in with a strong hand and doing good work where necessary.

Well now, I must close now for the time, I may be able to write another letter and send with this, or I may find an opportunity of sending it out immediately. Whether in time or not, you are all assured of my very best love and wishes for a Merry Christmas and a happy and prosperous New Year. Be sure and take care of yourselves and your appetites at this treacherous season.

With love and kisses to all from
Will

15 December 1898
Rant Avenue
Atlin City B.C.

My dear Lill (and all)

There is a New Zealander going out today and has offered to post a letter for me, so I am going to chance it and send a few lines. It is all chance whether my letters reach you. I sent out long ones about a month or six weeks ago by a very old man, but news has arrived that his party had a terrible mishap. The old man had to throw away his blankets and everything to make a dash for help to escape being frozen to death. Whether he retained the letters or not I cannot say. Another member only saved his legs by taking off his coat and wrapping it round them, whilst a third man had to be left behind on the trail. The poor fellow was discovered by the Police who were sent to his assistance, wrapped in the old man's blankets and nearly an idiot. He has lost all his fingers and toes and lies in a bad state I hear.

I have just come back from a very hard trip to O'Donnell River. Was away twelve days, but the water was so swift that a few days mild weather made the ice too rotten to be pleasant and over and over again we had mishaps. But I think we may congratulate ourselves on having secured good claims on three rivers whilst away. My claim on O'Donnell River I have named the 'Lily of Bridport'. I also staked a claim for Nellie but do not know whether the law will allow me to hold it. I am told that if I take out a licence for her, it is alright, according to B.C. law. Williams also staked for his wife. I think the claims will prove very rich, but could not give them a fair testing as water broke in on us and flooded us out before we got to bed-rock. We did not care for the place where the Dr. has staked, so went three miles above. We got down nine feet, finding colours all the way and the last pan was the most encouraging of all. 'Canyon Creek' (what the Doc will know as 'Carriboo Creek') also appears to be good. We also discovered another creek which we named 'Britannia Creek' and where we staked a Discovery claim. If anyone sees O'Donnell before he leaves England will you tell him that we could not stake for him as arranged, owing to a blinding snowstorm, and the ice became so treacherous that we dare not return the day following. We were unable to test the creek at all owing to want of water, the creek at this season being absolutely dry. But we hope to return again in about a month and intend to place him next to Discovery, if no one else is before us.

There was a magnificent treat awaiting me when I got back. It wasn't a letter, but the next best thing - a Methodist Times which Nellie had sent, dated the 27th October. It was a large number and I have gained lots of news from it. I see Bennett is gone to Hastings; Milner is at Sandown, I of Wight; Norton at Wimbledon or that circuit; Goodman at Barry Road again, and Bennetts colleague appears to be dear old Nettleton, a Barry Road acquaintance, he being at Mostyn Road when first I went to Barry. Then again, it appears that war is imminent between France and England. But I don't suppose the froggies would be such fools. Hughes is president I see. There is a full account of the great Birmingham Convention and full report of proceedings of the 20th Century Fund Committee. It all came like a breath from the other world. That makes the third communication I have had from the outer world since March 10th and I had to pay 25 cents for that paper. I would have paid 25 shillings without a murmur. There are tons of mail waiting at Bennett I hear, but it is so dangerous to get there that it is out of the question; but a man has gone out to try and bring some in and I have promised to pay him 2 shillings for every letter he brings me. I hope it will be fifty. There must be quite that number knocking about for me somewhere I am sure.

If you were to come to Atlin now, you would see the following notice posted all over the town:

"To all whom it may concern.

All Britishers resident in Atlin and district who would care to meet on Christmas night and keep up Christmas in the good 'Old Country' style are requested to call on the undersigned not later than Saturday 17th inst."

W.T.White
Rant Avenue Secy. to Committee of Arrangements.

There are about 30 here who will be present and we mean to have a good old time. Apples, nuts, oranges, etc. will be absent, but we are going to have a good spread, moose meat, plum pudding, mince pies, blancmanges etc. Dinner at 9 o/clock, toasts etc., and after midnight we will have a jolly good time. The ladies are going to cook for us and wait upon us. There are three married women here who are really ladies. It seems so strange to come across refinement in this out of the world spot, but I enjoy to get away and spend an evening with them and their lucky husbands now and again.

The weather is not nearly so severe now, though we have had continuous snow now for the last few days. But the snow here is not like our English snow, it is far drier.

I shall be thinking of the inglenook the next few days I assure you. What a vast difference to last Christmas! You would never imagine it. I am told that I have aged considerably. I think it must be true for I have never shaved since last March and am a sight for men and angels to weep over. I shall be glad to get to Skagway next month as I am sadly in need of a pair of unmentionables. The trousers I have on are the only pair I possess in the world, and they are becoming more holy than righteous, albeit they are thick, warm and comfortable. A cheap pair here would probably cost about £4.10s.0d or £5. Things are awful expensive, you know. Sugar is dear. None to be got under 2/- a lb. and most other things are on a par. Still it doesn't make much difference to us for we have practically all we want in the eating line, for the next three or four months.

Well, Lill, I don't know that I can write more now. I am thinking, if my claims turn out well, of leaving here next Autumn and getting Dad to join me at New York or Friscoe, from whence we can pass on to Honolulu, Fiji Islands, Australia, Ceylon, Red Sea, Egypt, Suez, Mediterranean, Naples, Switzerland, Paris, London and Bridport before Christmas. Rather an ambitious programme, but quite within the bounds of possibility. I should love to do the trip with Father, and if it is any way possible it will have to be done.

Day after

Hurrah! It never rains but it pours!! By some unaccountable and mysterious chance I have found in this camp a newspaper dated 23rd August and the name of it is Pulman's Weekly News. Just imagine how my heart jumped when I spied the name. How eagerly I scanned the pages for the word Bridport. There was an account of West Bay Regatta, but I was sorry to see that rain interferred with the enjoyment. A boat capsized I see. I notice the announcement of Simmond's death. And there is a long account of old Broadley and Earl de la Warr being prosecuted for Contempt of Court in connection with the Hooley business. I hope Father is straight with Broadley. He appears to be another Stansfield's kind. By the way Stansfield left for England a few days since, I believe. He is quite a villain enough to write blackmailing or threatening letters, but if he should do so just gool him at once, and in any case don't take notice of a word he may say. He is a consummate liar, we have found. Dr O'Donnell will tell you a thing or two about him, if any of you are so fortunate as to see him. But I must dry up. Glad I found that paper though.

Your affect.

Will

Best love to Father, Mother, Flo, Harold and Bert. Bring 'em home a nugget next year.

7

First Christmas at Atlin City

Boxing Night /98
Atlin City, B.C.

My dear Lill (and all)

I have had you all in my thoughts during the last four or five days and had I been fool enough to mope and get homesick, I should have suffered a great deal by drawing too vivid a comparison between my present Christmas and that of last year. But resolutely determined to allow of no such tomfoolery I have entered heart and soul into a plan for spending Christmas which has succeeded as only success can succeed. As I told you in my last letter the English boys in camp (about 40) decided to join in preparing, eating and digesting a Christmas Dinner that should be a credit to the dear old country we love so well. One never realises one's affection for the land of our birth until separated by 8000 miles or so. For the purpose of getting up this Dinner, a Committee of the Boys was formed, and your humble 'little brodder' had the honour of being elected Secretary. For weeks preparations had been made for having as good a time as circumstances of our environment would permit, and amongst all resident of the 'old sod' the watchword has been 'Christmas of the good old sort in the good old way'. But I had better start at the beginning and tell you how we kept Christmas in Atlin.

Christmas Eve was a beautiful night. The moon shone forth in the heavens with a lustre altogether unusual even in this country with its glorious atmosphere, whilst the snow underfoot was as crisp and dry as a well-cooked biscuit. At midnight seven of us repaired to Dr. Talbot's Drug Stores at the foot of Rant Avenue for the purpose of inaugurating the first Christmas in Atlin by singing a selection of carols in various parts of the town. Punctual to the minute we sallied forth and in a few minutes the beautiful hymn 'Christians Awake' floated upward through the frosty air. Mr. Anderson, an American, and his young bride from sunny California, were evidently taken by surprise, but greatly appreciated the singing which was really of a very high order. As you know, I am no singer myself and my presence in the group was more that of a friend than a songster but my partner Williams is a grand alto and Dr. Talbot a good bass and the other four very fair singers indeed. At Mrs Wright's we sang 'Noel' and at Mr and Mrs Ogilvie's 'Adeste Fidelis' and 'Christians Awake'. Here nothing would do but we must come in and have supper - hot coffee, cocoanut cake and real marmalade (Keillers). Our next visit was to the Atlin Hotel and here again we had to go inside and warm up. Williams and I being teetotal boys, accepted cigars instead of toddy. From here we went to Mr and Mrs Davis on 2nd Street and here again we found a big supply of coffee, cake and tarts awaiting us. But we had to refuse this time, for at this rate of progress we should never cover the city area. Opposite the Opera House (about the size of our Drill Hall) on Discovery Avenue we gave Mr and Mrs Kinney a couple of carols and in acknowledgement Mr Kinney is presenting us with a box of 590 cigars, which are selling at 1/- each here now. Mr and Mrs Gregory from Australia were then visited and finally we called upon Mr Jameson, and here were regaled with hot cocoa till we felt like bursting up altogether. Well as it was half past three we looked longingly towards our beds and soon our bodies followed our glances and we were sleeping contentedly in the arms of Morpheus. On Christmas Day we were congratulated on all sides and by none more heartily than the Yankies, to whom carol singing came as a welcome novelty, as it appears that the Waits are almost unknown in the States.

Well Christmas Day was a busy day for me, and indeed for all of the committee, for we were determined that the Dinner should be a knock-out and indeed it was. I should like Father to have been there. He would have found it so novel and fresh. Each member had to bring his own knife, fork, spoon, plate and cup and a candle and as there were forty present we were able to have fifteen or twenty candles on the table at once, which brilliant illumination lighted up the cabin in grand style. The log house lent for the occasion was 20 x 20 and the walls were nicely decorated with guns, revolvers, greenery and the Canadian flag. At nine o'clock punctual, each man was in his seat and the excitement ran high when Dr J F Phillip of Aberdeen took the chair. Now I think I had better give you a list of the various things we bought and which the ladies had kindly cooked and made into pies, puddings, stews etc. etc.

21lbs Moose (an animal about the size of a large cow)	40 lbs flour	2 tins marmalade
	6 lbs mince	4 lbs prunes
	10 lbs sugar	4 lbs apples
2 lbs Moose Tongue	5 lbs butter	1 cup molassess
4 lbs suet	1 bottle celery salt	half pint brandy
8 grouse	5 lbs cheese	1 pt run
2 rabbits	3 boxes spices	2 dozen eggs
3 lbs bacon	9 lbs currants	1 tin mustard
1 lb salt pork	5 lbs raisins	1 tin pepper
15 lbs potatoes	1 lb tea	
3 tins milk	1 lb coffee	

Now you can see that when these things are made into the various things, such as plum pudding, mince pies, cakes, stewed fruits etc., it must mean a meal vastly different to beans and bacon, almost our daily food for the last few months. Guess then our excitement as the great dinner drew nigh. Some of us hadn't eaten all day so that our appetites might be sharpened and that we might carry away as much of the good things as possible. Well Lill that dinner lasted 2 hours and a half. Two hours and a half of solid eating without a break, except to get wind, and one poor chap managed to get what he called his second wind and by jove it was terrible the tragic way in which that fellow started in on his second dinner. For the first hour of the dinner scarcely a sound could be heard save when some poor fellow heaved a sigh of contentment and happiness whilst pausing to get his plate replenished.

But such a state of things could not last forever and after eleven o'clock the intensity of purpose written on every face began to give place to a benign and self-complacent affability that soon became as hilarious and genial as only can be found in a John Bull party - after dinner, and the meal that began with a rigid silence ended amidst laughter and jollity that sounded as English as one could wish.

The men now retired to the Drug Stores for a chat and a smoke whilst the ladies sat down to their dinner, which by the way they well deserved, for it was no mean task to keep forty hungry men supplied for 2 and a half hours. Meanwhile I installed myself as head cook and bottle washer and washed and wiped all the plates, cups and knives, forks, spoons etc. By the way I had forgotten to mention that I wore my best black coat for the occasion - the first time since leaving Vancouver. It was a treat to feel that I looked respectable again and if I had only a collar with me I should have been in heaven. Still such luxuries are unknown amongst miners and there were only three men who could wear a collar, amongst all those present, and they ran a considerable risk for it was seriously considered whether we should fine them 5 dollars each for breaking the miners etiquette. I flatter myself, Nell would have considered me as charming as ever, with my blue jersey and black tail coat. Well, at midnight we reassembled and the toast The Queen was drunk with hearty goodwill amidst the squealing of the band playing the National Anthem, the band consisting of a violin, clarionette, and guitar. Then followed songs, comic and otherwise with stump speeches, recitations, etc. and the following toasts at intervals -

    Great Britain & Colonies
    Navy, Army & Reserve Forces
    Absent Friends at Home
    Atlin District
    The Ladies
    Our American Cousins

These toasts provoked some good speeches and most present felt a lump in their throat whilst we drank to Absent Friends at Home. But we all sang or tried to sing a verse of Home Sweet Home, some of us shouting our loudest in order to keep something like moisture from our eyes. Well, we soon banished all unnerving thoughts and the fun ran high, song after song was called for and it was not until half past six in the morning that any one thought of retiring. At that time the party ended with Auld Lang Syne & God Save the Queen and so ended a Christmas Dinner and party that will live long in the memories of all present.

Everyone was satisfied and delighted and it will serve as a topic for endless discussion in the camp. Just fancy, from nine in the evening till half past six in the morning. Of course, it was a scratch team - men of all sorts and conditions, but there was perfect gentlemanliness throughout and not one word or action that the most prudish could have regretted, and the ladies present - only three - were able to stay till the finish and have a real good time. Well, Lill, this in brief is the account of how we spent Christmas at Atlin, and I think you will admit that we did well and no-one will blame us for making this supreme effort to banish sad and anxious thoughts from our hearts, Amen.

Here endeth the first Christmas. I wonder when I shall get a letter describing your own Christmas. The main features I can easily imagine such as the roast beef, plum puddings, goose, etc., but the details of course are beyond me. I expect you spent a nice quiet Christmas and did much the same as usual. Did you have my little Girl with you? I have pictured her amongst you in all my visions of home lately. I am beginning to feel very anxious about you all now. August 5th was the date of the last letter and it is getting quite time I heard again. The man 'Big Jack' who went out specially for letters is not back yet and I scarcely expect he will be back before New Year, but when he comes I feel quite certain he will bring me a big mail. I wish I was sure of your receiving this. A man has promised to post this for me, but it is doubtful whether he will get through safely.

There is and has been a terrible tale in the camp for several days that Dr. O'Donnell (who had several letters for you) has never been seen since leaving here, but that his tracks show that he wandered from the trail and everything points to his having been eaten by wolves. I devoutly hope it is untrue. The whole camp is very despondent about it though, as unfortunately everything seems to point that way. God grant it is untrue, but if so, four brave men have passed away. But I can't and will not believe it. At home, around your snug fires you cannot know of the dangers the brave men run who attempt to get out of the country at this time of the year. I would no more think of leaving Atlin during November and December than I would fly, as only men of the soundest, hardest and most enduring constitutions can do it with safety. I flatter myself that I am pretty tough just now, but I don't intend to test it in that way.

People tell me I am getting very fat and look as though I am 'home fed' rather than existing on beans and bacon. I think myself there is some truth in the impeachment but as it is about three months since I have seen anything in the shape of a mirror I cannot say for certain. I have never shaved since leaving Vancouver so far as I can remember and the effect is most excruciating.

I have been lucky the last few weeks in managing to get quite a lot of reading material. First came the Methodist Times, then the Pulman's Weekly News for August 26th and the Review of Reviews for August and now a very interesting novel of Wm. Black's Sabina Zembla. If you have it in the library you might get it as I think you could care for it, also the Princess of Thule by the same author. The days are soon over lasting only from eight to three at the very most, so you see we have much time for reading. You might occasionally send out the weekly edition of the Times as now a man is going regularly to Bennett for mail I shall be pretty certain to get it.

Referring to that Christmas Party of ours, it was just grand to taste anything in the pastry line again - real mince pies and plum cakes once more. The Committee decided to allow Dr. Talbot to take everything left over as he has worked so hard for the success. Williams and I are great pals with the old doctor, and nothing would suffice but we must go halves with him, so that we are well stocked with mince pies, cakes, rabbit stews, bread etc. Still they are not Mother's cake and mince pies. This chief will be glad when he can taste a bit of Mother's cake again.

I have just heard that a search party has gone out to try and find news of O'Donnell but I am afraid the case looks very black, as the district where the accident is said to have occurred is known to be infested with wolves of the worst kind. In passing through it last Spring I saw two myself, come down to within 200 yards of the trail in broad daylight; and of course with the snow being deep on the ground at this time, and running in packs, they are just ravenous and would attack anything.

Poor Doctor, he was one of the nicest fellows I ever met, and had promised to call and see Nell whilst in London and bring me news of her when he returned in the Spring. Well, we will hope for the best, and not entirely give up hope.

Now take care of yourself, Lill dear, and look after the whole bag of tricks till I can get home and relieve you of some of the responsibility.

Will xxxxxxxxxx

Day after New Year's Day 1899

Dear Dad,

Yesterday was one of the finest days you ever saw. The sun shone brightly with the thermometer 20° below zero, and the lake, which the previous evening was all open running water, was covered with 2 inches of ice from one side to the other (about 8 miles) and from end to end (about 75 miles). Many put on skates and spent the day skating but they did not go more than ten or a dozen yards from the shore. Towards dusk two fine big stalwart fellows with their bodies more full of whisky than their heads full of brains, started off in spite of all warning to walk across to the first island - probably about 250 yards from the shore. We thought they would get across safely after a while, but when only about 50 yards from the island the ice cracked and the poor fellows were in 40 feet of water with the thermometer 25° below zero. Like lightning two brave fellows caught up a canoe from the bank and running it over the ice, one on either side of it, ran it into the hole jumping into the boat as it struck the water.

They hauled the first man into the boat and had nearly got the other one in, (they were brothers by the way) when the first and eldest lurched forward, and the next thing we saw was the four fellows in the water and the canoe bottom up.

Oh Dad it was terrible! The horror of it all kept some of us rooted to the ground. But there were some who retained their heads and in less time than it takes to write it, four more brave fellows with two more boats were skimming over the ice to the rescue. Ropes were connecting the boats with the shore, but long before one of them reached the drowning men, the other had hopelessly broken through the ice and had to be abandoned. But the other reached the hole in safety and amidst breathless silence we could just see in the dusk that three bodies were being lifted into the boat which was then rapidly drawn ashore. The fourth had sunk - and on New Year's Day! Death had claimed his first victim in Atlin and through drink! The poor fellow was drowned whilst 200 people stood 200 yards off helpless. Oh it was pitiable. What an awful thought, for the brother that is left, too!!! They cut through the ice today and found the body. I was one of the jury at the inquest. Asked as to what condition they were in when they started, the surviving brother made the following Yankee but pathetic yet condemnatory admission - "I guess we were intoxicated". So the New Year has opened with gloom in the new Gold Fields. I hope it will be a lesson to everyone to keep away from the drink. I hate it more and more! The further I go, the more damning seems its effects. I'll have none of it.

Now I must dry up as this letter is going to be taken out tomorrow and I have another to finish.

Take care of yourself now Daddie,

Yours longingly,

Will.

8

Changes in Occupation

The year so tragically begun, proved to be a year of disappointment for Will. Further letters from him have been lost but in an article about him, written in 1966, it is recorded that the optimistic hopes of him and his partner were dashed. Despite their strenuous efforts during the following months they failed to discover significant quantities of gold on their claims in the Atlin area and had to turn their hands to other means of support. A few others were more fortunate and the Atlin area is said to have produced 25 million dollars worth of gold.

First they started a haying business on the shores of Lake Tagish where they baled and sold fodder at $100 a ton. But sadly for them completion of the railway, then under construction between Whitehorse and Skagway, put an end to this venture. They next tried chopping and selling lumber and then ran a roadhouse to feed and house travellers along the trail. Finally they broke up the partnership and, in the spring of the following year, Will arrived in Whitehorse rich in experience but with only 50 cents in his pocket. There he survived by undertaking a few odd jobs until in June he had a stroke of luck.

What happened he recorded in an article which he wrote in 1938 and which was published in the house magazine of the Canadian Bank of Commerce under the title 'Upper Yukon Reminiscences'.

It read as follows...

'It was a beautiful summer morning such as old Yukoners love to recall. The daily train from Whitehorse, over the White Pass to the sea-board at Skagway, was on the move from the depot when Mr Lay, the Bank Manager at Whitehorse, approached me as I stood watching the receding cars and asked me if I was free to take on a job. With the opening of the navigation season, and the large rush from the outside, the branch had been swamped with work, and in view of the expected arrival of the Bank's Inspector it was desirable to get caught up; he could not offer me a permanent position but would appreciate assistance for a month or six weeks.

Despite the fact that I had left England with the avowed intention of avoiding an indoor life and especially anything to do with banking, I was financially lean enough to accept Mr Lay's S.O.S. Within an hour, then, behold me behind the counter at the White Horse branch, a temporary member of the staff of The Canadian Bank of Commerce, diligently sorting and filing accumulated correspondence and vouchers.

In due course the Inspector paid his visit and before leaving offered me a six months' engagement. At the expiration of this time nothing was said regarding the termination of my engagement, and after some eighteen months an application to be placed upon the permanent staff, supported by the recommendation of Mr. Lay's successor, Mr Nourse, resulted in definitely binding me to a career I had left England to avoid.

Followed three years of initiation into the mysteries of Canadian banking. Whitehorse, at the head of navigation on the Yukon, was a busy point in the early years of the century and the business handled was varied and intriguing. Prior to the opening of the river for the summer months the town swarmed with a transient population eager to reach Dawson at the earliest possible moment to avail themselves to the full extent of the short summer season, and in the fall, before the freeze-up, the population would again increase by the arrival of thousands, all following the geese southwards, for the duration of the winter.

The Bank staff of four ran a Mess, and Mr. Nourse, an old Dawsonite and an ideal host, loved to extend the hospitality of the Mess to his sourdough friends of '98 and '99. As a result, I had the privilege of meeting many of the men whose names were foremost in the pioneer days of the Yukon, and among the most pleasant recollections of those days are the memories of these old-timers 'swapping' yarns of their experiences on the Trail and recalling incidents of the hectic times through which they had so recently passed and to which they had, in no small measure, largely contributed.

Under a regime where lavish hospitality was the rule, it is not surprising that our Mess account was chronically in the red. The situation was accentuated by an extravagent Jap chef, who was obsessed with the idea that the entire capitalization of the Bank was behind him. Indeed, on one occasion from the dining room I overhead a conversation in the adjoining kitchen between the cook and a fellow countryman who officiated in a similar capacity for the Officers's Mess of the N.W.M. Police. Our cook was busily cracking eggs for an angel cake and his visitor was expostulating at the recklessness with which they were being used. "Too much expensive," he said, "too much expensive." "That's alright," exclaimed our cook, "quite alright. Ten million capital." Small wonder then that, with our Mess account heavily overdrawn, our hospitable Manager was ultimately forced to ask for an appropriation. The correspondence that ensued was an anxious one for the younger members of the Mess, but Charlie Nourse was adept at marshalling all relevant facts, and his case was perhaps won when he reminded the Department that "it should not be overlooked that one of the members of the Mess is Mr deGex, whose abilities as a trencherman are known throughout the service."

Life in Whitehorse in those days was never dull, and the presence of a large detachment of the N.W.M. Police, under Major Snyder, contributed much to the life of the community. Many of the officers were accompanied by their wives and families, as also were the executive heads of the railroad and river transportation services. There were numerous stores and many of the merchants were family men. The Judiciary, Public Works Department, Government Telegraphs, Customs, churches, medical and hospital services each accounted for other families, so there was no lack of social life in the community and spare time passed most pleasantly. Sports, both summer and winter, were keenly followed and contested. On account of the long hours of daylight in the summer, tennis and baseball were enjoyed to the limit, and in winter, skating, sleigh rides and curling were popular pastimes. ... '

In the meantime Nell, Will's bride to be, was at home in Charmouth awaiting his return. Although hopes of an early return with a fortune had expired by the time Will joined the bank she still hoped for his return within the promised four years and started to plan her wedding. She made dresses for herself and for her four bridesmaids. Sadly, however, Will discovered, not long after he had been confirmed in his appointment at the Bank, that employees were not allowed to marry until their salary reached a figure higher than that which he was receiving. So, at the first opportunity, he returned to Bridport to visit his family and discuss the situation with Nell.

Hoping that promotion might soon solve their marriage problem Nell agreed that he should return to his banking career and the targeted date for their wedding was extended. The dresses were put aside and Will returned to Whitehorse.

Promotion came in 1905 when, following a brief spell in the bank at Vancouver, Will was appointed teller at the branch at Penticton and a few months later at Fernie. There in 1906, eight years after he had set out for Canada and still not earning enough to marry, his patience ran out and Will told the bank that, even if they fired him, he was going to get married. Instead he was promoted to accountant and he quickly sent word to Nell to come to Canada. She left Charmouth almost at a moment's notice and sailed for Canada with a new wedding dress in her luggage. Will, having completed arrangements at a church in Montreal, travelled to Quebec to meet the boat but, because of rough weather, it was 4 days late in arriving. Arriving back in Montreal they booked in at an hotel and set out for the church to make fresh arrangements for their wedding. They arrived just half an hour before the minister was due to leave for holiday and so, with Will's leave running out, they decided they must marry there and then!

The ceremony took place in the minister's parlour with his housekeeper as witness. Will was wearing his old tweed knickers and

Nell in her well worn travelling clothes. Her second wedding dress was still unpacked in her trunk at the hotel. They returned to the hotel, had a meal of sausages for their wedding breakfast, and next day left to return to Fernie.

Will and Nell shortly after their marriage

9

THE BANK ROBBERY AT SKAGWAY

In March of the following year Will was appointed manager of the bank at Skagway. It was 9 years since he had first set foot in the town.

The bank there had, some few years earlier, when Will was ledger keeper at Whitehorse, been the scene of a hold-up which gave rise to a bizarre chain of events. Will later recorded an account of these.

His story went as follows: ...

The manager at the Skagway branch was away on a hunting trip and our accountant, Mr de Gex, was sent to take charge. Just before he arrived, a man walked into the bank and pulling a gun from his pocket, asked the ledger keeper at the counter, a Mr Wallace, if he knew what it was.

Mr Wallace, a level headed chap who had only recently returned from the South African war, grinned and said, "It looks like a gun." "Right," said the man and taking something from his left hand pocket, he repeated the question. Wallace recognised what it was and somewhat scared said, "Well, it looks like dynamite." "Right again," said the man, "and unless you hand over $30,000 I'll blow the place up." Wallace walked towards the safe in the corner of the office. But as he reached it he sprang towards a door at the back and shouted to his companions to duck. The robber was startled and fired. His bullet missed both men and drilled a hole through a stanchion at the corner of the tellers' cage. But the concussion exploded the dynamite blowing everything to pieces including the man himself.

Wallace was uninjured but his companion, who had ducked his head into a little book safe on the shelf beside him, suffered damage to his hearing. One other casualty was the bank's solicitor who was blown back into the street showered with broken glass as he was about to enter the bank.

Our accountant, Mr de Gex, arrived on the scene about an hour after the robbery and took charge. On his return he told us of the difficult time they had had in clearing up the mess. There had been a huge canister of gold dust on the counter and this had been blown over and scattered, so they had rigged up sluice boxes in the street and sifted all the debris from the building. They made such a good job of it that they ended up with an ounce of gold more than the books of the bank showed! They had collected gold dust which had slipped through the floor boards over the years since the bank opened.

Mr de Gex also told us how, as chief mourner and representative of the bank, he had attended the funeral of the robber. And he went on to confess that at the service he had had some difficulty maintaining a proper degree of respect. At the instigation of the local doctor, the pair of them had been up to the mortuary the previous night, removed the robbers remains, and filled the coffin with brickbats and sand, so that when the parson uttered the words 'dust to dust' they found it difficult to supress a grin.

In support of this story Mr de Gex had returned with one of the robber's thumbs, preserved in a bottle of alcohol and he charged us 50 cents for a 25 cent drink of whisky for the privilege of inspecting it.

I remembered all this when some few years later I was promoted to the post of manager at Skagway. The story had always intrigued me and I was curious to know what had actually happened to the body.

So I started making enquiries. The doctor's practice had changed hands more than once during the years and it took me some time to come to the conclusion that the remains of the robber were possibly

The Bank after the attempted robbery

in the keeping of the local photographer, a man whom I knew quite well. So I went to see him and suggested that if he did have the remains it was foolish to keep them as he might get into trouble. He admitted that he did have them and that they were out in his woodshed.

He also confessed that for the past 18 months he'd been scared to go out to the shed after dark. So I suggested that it might be better if the remains were returned to the care of the bank and I offered to take them with me. We went out to the woodshed and there was a double row of wood all stacked up. He pulled down one row to get into the back row and away at the back he fished out an old gunny sack. "There he is," he said. Well I got hold of it and lifted it up but it was so mouldy that it started to break. So he fetched a new sack and we put the old one in it. I slung it over my shoulder and walked up town with it back to the bank. There I decided that the best thing to do was to take them to an old friend, another doctor. He was busy writing at his desk as I went in. He looked up, said "Good morning White" and went on writing. After a minute or two I walked to the centre of his office and up-ended the sack on the floor. Hearing the noise he turned round, saw the bones on the floor, and said "For God's sake boy, what have you been up to? You must have been to the cemetery very early this morning."

I told him what the bones were. They were in a poor state of preservation, worm- eaten and mildewed, but he picked out one or two of interest to him and I took the skull. The rest we gathered up and threw into his stove so in the end much of the robber was actually cremated. I took the skull back to the bank where it stayed until the bank closed in 1910. Just before leaving I took it to the local dentist and made him a present of it. He placed it on his mantleshelf and that was the last I heard of it.

10

CONCLUSION AND REFLECTIONS

After leaving Skagway, Will was appointed Manager of the bank at Cumberland, BC, where he spent the next five years. He was then transferred to Virden, Manitoba and in 1917 to Moncton, BC. By then he and Nell had acquired a family of one son and two daughters. After six years in Moncton he became Manager at Woodstock, Ontario and then in 1926 he returned to Vancouver as the bank's Custodian of Securities. He retired in 1932. By then his family had grown up and he had thoughts of returning to Bridport to live in retirement there. But, after spending a winter with his parents in Bridport, the absence of central heating and other modern conveniences to which he and Nell had become accustomed quickly changed his mind and they returned to Vancouver. One of his hobbies was stamp collecting and in an address he gave to the British Columbian Philatelic Society in 1952 he looked back on his Yukon Experiences.

"I have never been a fluent speaker and, since I have been somewhat pitch-forked into the lime-light, must ask you to excuse my shortcomings. I feel this more especially since, in order to speak of Experiences in the Yukon, it necessarily means that I have largely to speak about myself – indeed to unfold the sad story of my life - or at least the period of four years that I spent in the hills of the

North before settling down to the hum-drum existence of a banker and learning to say NO with the proper emphasis. These years were so crowded with experience that I can only sketch briefly a few of the highlights that will afford some glimpses of my chequered past.

I arrived in Vancouver in March 1898, just past 23 years of age and very green, from London, England, where for some five years I had been in a junior branch of the Civil Service at the head office of the Post Office Savings Bank. Vancouver in those days - 54 years ago - was a very different city to what we have today. Cordova was the chief business street; Hastings Street West was beginning to come into its own, but Granville Street was still chiefly vacant lots and largely bush beyond Robson Street, as were the blocks approaching Stanley Park, to the west. The population of the city at that time was less than 20,000 and was densest east of Carrall Street. As I remember it the trend was towards Grandview and Mount Pleasant, and Major Matthews informs me that at that time bears and an occasional cougar were still bothering the children attending the Mount Pleasant school.

It is beyond me to give an adequate description of conditions that were encountered in that 35 miles over the White Pass between Skagway and Lake Bennett, the navigable head-waters of the Yukon River. The cruelty to animals was something terrible. It is no use harrowing you with details of these acts of brutality, and it would mean endless repetition, for the whole trail was strewn with dead animals of all kinds. I remember on one occasion, packing a heavy load on my back and being clamorous for a drink, I threw myself on my knees and lapped a fill of water from a small rivulet that ran close to the trail. Satisfied, I arose and saw that practically the whole stream was gurgling through the putrid remains of a horse lying a few yards above me.

No-one has better absorbed and described, both in verse and in prose, the atmosphere of the early Yukon days than Robert Service.

I knew him well, for we worked together for a while. I have an autographed copy of his work he sent me, "Songs of a Sourdough". It might be of interest to explain that a "Sourdough" is the proud title given to one who has seen the ice form on the Yukon River, in the Fall, and has remained in the country until it has broken up and gone away again in the Spring. Until you have qualified in this way, to the Northerners you are only a "Cheechako".

W. White

The Law of the Yukon

*This is the law of the Yukon, and
ever she makes it plain;*

*Send not your foolish and feeble;
send me your strong and sane—*

*Strong for the red rage of battle;
sane, for I harry them sore.*

*Send me men girt for the combat,
men who are grit to the core;*

*Swift as the panther in triumph,
fierce as the bear in defeat,*

*Sired of a bulldog parent, steeled
in the furnace heat.*

*Send me the best of your breeding,
lend me your chosen ones;*

*Them will I take to my bosom, them
will I call my sons;*

*Them will I gild with my treasure,
them will I glut with my meat;*

*But the others – the misfits, the
failures – I trample under my feet.*

*Dissolute, damned and despairful,
crippled and palsied and slain,*

*Ye would send me the spawn of your
gutters – Go! take back your spawn again.*

Robert Service